GREECE

*A la mémoire
de Bernard Jaoul*

1. Athènes. L'Acropole vue de l'Est. De gauche à droite: la Pinacothèque, les Propylées,   *1. Athen.*
le temple d'Athéna Niké, le Parthénon. Au-dessous des Propylées: la Porte Beulé.

The Acropolis seen from the east.

1. *Athen. Ostansicht der Akropolis.*

2. L'Olympieion et
l'Acropole, le soir.

2. The Olympieion and
the Acropolis at night.

2. Olympieion und Akropolis
am Abend.

GREECE

By Jeanne and Georges Roux

Translated by
Lionel and Miriam Kochan

With 264 heliogravure illustrations by
Bernard Aury, Spyros Méletzis,
Emile Sérafis & Nick Stournaras, etc.

NEW YORK
OXFORD UNIVERSITY PRESS
1965

First published in French by
B. ARTHAUD (PARIS & GRENOBLE)
under the title
LA GRÈCE

ENGLISH TEXT © 1958, 1965 NICHOLAS VANE (PUBLISHERS) LTD

PLATES PRINTED IN FRANCE
TEXT PRINTED IN GREAT BRITAIN

CONTENTS

LIST OF ILLUSTRATIONS

All photographs, unless otherwise stated, are by Bernard Aury and are the exclusive property of Editions Arthaud. Material from Michael Audrain, S. Méletzis (37, 38, 39), and N. Stournaras (50, 54, 55, 73, 123), is also the exclusive property of Editions Arthaud

28. NATIONAL MUSEUM OF ATHENS. Large funeral amphora in geometric style from the Dipylon (Ceramic Cemetery). Representation of a funeral lament. Height about 5 feet 2 inches. 800 BC

29. MUSEUM OF ARGOS. Geometric bowl from Argos. Second half of the eighth century BC (*photograph by G. Roux*)

30. NATIONAL MUSEUM OF ATHENS. Funeral lecythus of Myrrhine in white marble. Height about 8 feet 9 inches. 420 BC (*photograph by E. Sérafis, Athens*)

31. NATIONAL MUSEUM OF ATHENS. The hoplite Aristion. Funeral stele. The work of Aristocles, found at Velanideza in Attica. Marble from the Pentelicon. Height about 8 feet. 510 BC (*photograph by E. Sérafis, Athens*)

32-33. NATIONAL MUSEUM OF ATHENS. Pedestal of the statue of a *couros:* bas-reliefs representing palaestra scenes (*photographs by Giraudon, Paris and E. Sérafis, Athens*)

34. NATIONAL MUSEUM OF ATHENS. Stone dumb-bells (*photograph by E. Sérafis, Athens*)

35. NATIONAL MUSEUM OF ATHENS. Bas-relief from Eleusis, known as the Great Goddesses. Demeter and Persephone giving a grain of corn to the young Triptolemus. Attica. Marble from the Pentelicon. Height about 7 feet 4 inches. 440-430 BC (*photograph by E. Sérafis, Athens*)

36. NATIONAL MUSEUM OF ATHENS. Stele from the Hoplitodrome. A warrior, running. Height about 3 feet 4 inches. 510 BC (*photograph by E. Sérafis, Athens*)

37-38-39. ACROPOLIS MUSEUM. *Cores* (*photographs by S. Méletzis, Athens*)

40. NATIONAL MUSEUM OF ATHENS. *Couros* of Volomandra. Marble. Height about 6 feet. 550 BC

41. NATIONAL MUSEUM OF ATHENS. *Couros* of Milo. Marble from Naxos. Ionic. Height about 7 feet 2 inches. About 550 BC

42. NATIONAL MUSEUM OF ATHENS. *Couros* of Anavyssos. Marble from Paros. Attic. Height about 6 feet 6 inches. 530 BC

43. NATIONAL MUSEUM OF ATHENS. Ephebe from Marathon. Bronze statue found in the sea near Marathon. Height about 4 feet 4 inches. Fourth century BC

44. NATIONAL MUSEUM OF ATHENS. Ephebe from Anticythera. Found in the sea near Anticythera Height about 6 feet 6 inches. About 340 BC (*photograph by E. Sérafis, Athens*)

45-46-47-48. NATIONAL MUSEUM OF ATHENS: ANCIENT JEWELLERY. From the Collection of Helene and Antoine Stathatos. 45. Mycenaean gold jewellery; 46. Laurel crown in gold. Hellenistic period; 47. Medallion decorated with a bust of Aphrodite. Hellenistic period; 48. Bracelets with serpents' heads. Hellenistic period (*photographs by E. Sérafis, Athens*)

49. BYZANTINE MUSEUM, ATHENS. Orpheus seated in front of a tree playing the lyre. Around him are animals. Symbol of Christ calling the pagans to him (?) (*photograph by N. Stournaras, Athens*)

CHAPTER I: ATHENS AND ATTICA

50. ARRIVAL AT ATHENS. Hadrian's Arch and the garden of Queen Amelia. In the background, Lycabettos (*photograph by N. Stournaras, Athens*)

51. ATHENS. Syntagma Square and the Acropolis at night

52-53. ATHENS. Evzones mounting guard in front of the royal palace

54. ATHENS. A street in modern Athens (*photograph by N. Stournaras, Athens*)

55. ATHENS. The Monastiraki quarter. Street of the 'babouches' (*photograph by N. Stournaras, Athens*)

56. ATHENS. *Coulouria* seller

57. ATHENS. Sponge merchant

58. ATHENS. Odeon of Herodes Atticus. On the hill of the Mouseion, the monument of Philopappos

59. ATHENS. The Acropolis seen from the Mouseion (Hill of the Muses)

60. ATHENS. The Parthenon

61. ATHENS. The Parthenon: east fronton. One of the horses of Selene and Dionysos

62. ATHENS. The Parthenon: west fronton. Fragments of statues (Cecrops and his daughter Aglauros?)

List of Illustrations

CHAPTER II: FROM ATHENS TO THE PELOPONNESE

CHAPTER III: DELPHI, PHOCIS AND EPIRUS

CHAPTER IV: SALONIKA, ATHOS, THASOS AND SAMOTHRACE

CHAPTER V: A VOYAGE TO THE ISLANDS

List of Illustrations

CHAPTER VI: RHODES

GREECE AND THE GREEKS

IT is only a short time since visitors to Greece were more often pilgrims than tourists. Hospitable but distant, rich in beauty but otherwise poor and uncomfortable, the country was visited by archaeologists and scholars seeking on her soil the remains of an antiquity they had learned to love in their college lecture rooms and desirous above all else of steeping themselves fervently in the source of their culture. 'Imagine me at Athens,' one of the first members of the French School of Athens wrote to his family in 1847, 'me at Athens, walking with my Plato at the Academy, on the bank of the Illisus, wandering from the prison where Socrates died to the tribune from which Demosthenes spoke, climbing the steps of the Propylaea almost on my knees, entering with a sort of religious veneration and profound sadness into the temple of the Parthenon, still so marvellously beautiful in its devastation. Is all this credible? What a dream! Let no one wake me up!'

Contemporary Greece was only interesting in relation to the Greece of former times. Her blue sky, her mountains, her sea were only a beautiful casket to contain her marble temples. Her sunshine was a sort of projector expressly provided throughout the day by providence to animate the play of light and shade on the fluted shafts of the columns. As for the inhabitants, they were the object of perpetual comparison with the idealized image every individual had formed of their ancestors. Imagining in quite good faith that the latter possessed noses which were the direct extensions of their foreheads, like the statues of Phidias, the visitor was disconsolate when he found the Grecian nose no longer existed in Greece. What evidence of decay! Evzones in kilts, sponge merchants, shepherds of Parnassus enveloped in great hairy capes—these were only the picturesque accessories of a journey. The essential aim still remained meditation over the ruins and a tête-à-tête with the great shades of antiquity. Thus Chateaubriand cried the name of Leonidas amidst the oleanders of Sparta and was surprised that the hero did not answer him.

Suddenly, times have changed. People used to come to Greece on pilgrimage. Now they come on holiday. The pilgrims—there are always some—are drowned in the wave of tourists who, in hundreds of thousands (over 600,000 in 1963), arrive from Europe and America in search of relaxation, light, heat and the picturesque. 'The temple is in ruins at the height of the promontory', but the visitor, shod in rubber flippers, prefers to honour Poseidon, god of the seas, directly in his own domain by diving into the translucent waters in pursuit of *merou*. Many, however, who arrive with only fairly nebulous memories of classical culture find, apart from modern Greece, a half-forgotten or unsuspected ancient Greece on the great archaeological sites, in the museums, in contact with the original monuments. This is a good way of approaching the past. It will then appear as it really is: not at all a dead epoch, a page of history which has been finally turned, but part of a truly living people, which, because they are the direct heirs to ancient Greece, makes modern Greece all the more comprehensible.

This radical change of perspective has resulted from the motor car, the aeroplane and also from the surprising speed with which Greece has learned to equip herself to receive the great movement of international tourism which has developed since the last war.

A short time ago, it was a distant country. Having arrived at Piraeus or on the platform of Athens station after a journey of several days, the traveller could only reach the famous sites by expending much time and energy. The network of communications was scant and often only gave a choice between one's own two legs or a mule. The temple of Bassae in the heart of Arcadia was three hours' walk from Andritsaina, and how many hours was Andritsaina from Athens! Delos was reached by a caique in company with cows and goats loaded to the sound of sharp slaps on the rump. In bad weather this Noah's Ark gave itself up to communal sea-sickness. At the stopping place, accommodation, though always hospitable, was of the most spartan type. A journey in Greece implied leisure and a course of asceticism enthusiastically accepted by pure philhellenes but scarcely tempting to people who primarily expected relaxation and comfort from a holiday.

All that belongs to yesterday. Today, apart from railway and boat, car and plane bring an ever-growing number of visitors to Greece. Athens airport, Ellenikon, is four or five hours' flight at the most from any one of the great European cities. Conscious of its new importance in tourist trade, the town planners have given their full attention to the splendid flowered boulevard which skirts the Gulf of Aegina and now joins the airport to the heart of the city. The gain in time is so considerable that some clubs organize weekend air-trips for their members. A Frenchman can leave his town on Friday evening and return on Monday having made the rapid acquaintance of Athens, Delphi and the great sites of Argolis. What would Jacob Spon, Huguenot doctor from Lyons, who visited Greece in the seventeenth century in the company of an Englishman, George Wheler, and left one of the first descriptions of the country to be published in French, say about all this?

Insignificant in 1950, tourism by car has developed spectacularly within a few years. The driver most frequently takes the almost uninterrupted line of motorways which join Turin to Athens across Italy and Yugoslavia. Others prefer to load their cars on to one of the two specially equipped 'ferry boats' which link Brindisi, Corfu, the ports of Igoumenitsa and Patras. Many combine the two itineraries, arrive via Yugoslavia and leave by Corfu, or the reverse. The usual shipping lines also undertake the transport of cars between Piraeus, Venice or Marseilles.

The heavy arrival of cars in Greece has opened to tourism regions which were previously little known because of their distance from Athens. Today, the visitor approaches Greece from these very regions. Landing at Igoumenitsa, he sees the wild mountain ranges of Epirus, Aetolia and Acarnania open up before him. If he crosses the Greek/Yugoslav frontier at Evzoni, he is at the door of Macedonia, of Thrace. He stops a while at Salonika and stays on the island of Thasos, where a short while ago no stranger set foot, other than archaeologist or mining engineer following his profession.

The network of roads which serves the great tourist routes is excellent and much less over-crowded than those of most European countries. A new coastal road reduces the distance between Athens and Salonika by some sixty miles. A motorway between Athens and Corinth accompanies the old small coast road, so picturesque but so tortuous. In the wild mountains of Epirus, good asphalt roadways have replaced the goat paths where the proud inhabitants of Souli, the Klephts of Zalongo, shot at the Albanians of Ali of Tebelen, pasha of Janina. Very convenient ferries between Rhion and Antirhion, in the Patras region, between Aigion and Itea, join the Peloponnese to Acarnania and Delphi across the Gulf of Corinth, freeing the driver of a long detour by the Isthmus.

Tourists arriving by boat or air can take advantage of the excellent road network by using one of the numerous de luxe motor coaches which cover the main archaeological sites every day under the escort of competent guides. If he is a resolute individualist, he can hire a car with or without driver at Athens and a caique at Piraeus for the islands. Apart from the regular boat services, numerous organized trips enable visits to be made comfortably and rapidly to the sites of the archipelago. The hurried tourist has recourse to internal air lines which in a maximum time of an hour and a half take him from Athens to Salonika, Cavalla, Alexandropolis, Mytilene, Rhodes, Crete, Janina and Corfu.

The Greek hotel trade, of recent creation, supplies all modern requirements and its standards are amongst the highest in Europe. Two chains of luxury hotels or motels, well designed architecturally, situated in dominant positions as at Nauplia or buried in flowers and foliage as at Epidaurus, give additional accommodation at stopping places from the north to the south of the country. New or re-modelled average hotels, tented villages, organized camping sites, enable a growing number of visitors every year to find fully satisfactory accommodation.

The catering is no less agreeable than the accommodation although gourmet standards must not be expected. We recommend the typically Greek inns where you go to the kitchen yourself and organize your own menu, choosing the dishes directly from the great casseroles shaped like flat discs. Grilled fish, fried *calamar*, lamb on skewers, sprinkled with origanum, lamb cooked in every conceivable way, vine leaves stuffed with rice, peppers, large black olives, are the most appreciated dishes. They are washed down either with *ouzo*—the Greek form of anisette or raki—with wine made from raisins, a favourite with philhellenic palates, or, in the last few years, with an excellent wine up to the best French standards, or with Fux beer—a transcription of the name of the German brewer, Fuchs—or quite simply with the fresh water which one accepts as a general rule in Greece. The recently founded fruit-juice industry near the orchards of Argolis and Acarnania is making rapid strides.

As there are no longer any problems of transport or accommodation, the visitor can devote all his time to reaping the rewards of a country particularly rich in natural beauties.

A glance at the geography of Greece is enough to explain the extreme variety of the countryside. The boundaries of her territories can be fixed by drawing an imaginary square on the map with sides about 375 miles long, and corners at Corfu, Crete, the town of Rhodes and around the Turkish town of Edirne. In this way, we have framed an area of 140,625 square miles: 89,834 square miles of coastline, 50,781 square miles of land, sprinkled with a multitude of islands and dented with mountains dropping into deep gulfs. This irregular landscape bathed in a luminous sea is the essence of the picturesque in the Greek countryside from the Macedonian peninsula of Chalcidice up to the Cretan Bay of Mirabella. None the less, differences in latitude and configuration modify the character of the countryside from north to south. In the north, Greece is mountainous and scarcely influenced by the Mediterranean. Epirus, Thessaly and Macedonia bristle with mountain ranges, the high wall of the Pindus Mountains and the blue pyramid of Mount Olympus where snow makes the winter even colder. Fir trees cover the slopes while planes cluster in the valleys by the banks of the rivers. There is abundant water with almost full-size rivers. The lakes of Janina and Castoria reflect houses with moss-covered slates. Edessa is surrounded by waterfalls which flow in fresh streams practically down to the streets. The plains of Thessaly and Macedonia are green in the springtime but after the harvest the wind whips up great clouds of dust over their deserted steppes stretching to the horizon. Greece here resembles central Europe. The ass of the Mediterranean is joined by the horse and bull, drawing long wooden four-wheeled carts.

In the south, Greece comes closer to the traditional idea: cleft mountains of chalk covered with rough moorland; grey rocks with dark patches of green oak trees, stone terraces with vines and olive trees on the slopes, stony paths which the heat fills with the perfume of thyme, mint and marjoram. It is the sunlit Greece of poor white houses; the people take their beds out on the flat roofs in the summer to catch every moment of nocturnal freshness. The sea is never far away, its ports humming with caiques and the air sometimes powdered with mist, sometimes so transparent that the horizon seems very near, suspended in space.

Admittedly, this diagrammatic picture must allow of some variations. The Peloponnese holds the fertile plains of Argolis and Messenia. There is green vegetation in the Arcadian valleys in the heart of summer, watered by icy torrents, and it often seems as if a bit of Jura has been transplanted to the Rhodian Mountains in the Aegean.

The country is richer in beauty than in natural resources. Mountains cover eighty per cent of the total surface. They divide up the country, making the problem of communications extremely difficult. Sources of energy are rare. Drilling for oil has started in some places. Very recently dams were built to supply power-stations; in future, huge metal pylons will tower above the Greek countryside. Mineral resources are scarce: silver-bearing lead was discovered at Laurion at the time of Miltiades, and there are bauxite, nickel and lignite at Euboea, iron at Thasos, pyrites in Ptolemais. Poorly provided as regards industry, Greece remains an agricultural and pastoral country; over half the population works in the fields. Macedonia lives from her tobacco, Thrace and Thessaly from corn. Cotton grows on the hot plain of Boeotia and seedless grapes in the hills of Corinth. There are olive trees and vines everywhere. Argolis, Messenia and the islands cultivate orange and lemon trees whose perfume is carried by the wind out over the sea and along the coast. Goats and sheep find their pastures on the most barren slopes, while the rich plains of Messenia, Argolis and Macedonia nourish horses and bovines as in olden times. The donkey fits into all types of countryside and is not even noticed.

Since the days of antiquity, the Greek has looked to the sea and to foreign countries for what his own land cannot offer; he is a merchant and a sailor. Not counting the innumerable caiques and fishing vessels, both of fish and sponges, the Greek merchant marine represents an important part of world tonnage. The shipbuilders make a fortune—often under the Panamanian flag—but they are later ready to pay back in kind what they save from harsh taxation, in the form of hospitals, museums, roads and stadiums. The same tactics are pursued by the rich traders, expatriated to Egypt, the Congo or America, perpetuating a tradition as old as the history of Greece herself. Finally, every year tourism increases the national revenues to a considerable extent.

Greece today is beautiful and varied enough to warrant a journey on her own account. It is quite possible to conceive of a tourist deciding to visit the country without entering a single museum. But that would be a shame. Bound to the past by a profound continuity, nothing explains contemporary Greece better than her history; and her history, in its turn, receives its most living commentary from the country.

Greek history opens with the splendid and mysterious Cretan preface.

19

Who were the Cretans? What language did they speak? There are many questions without answers. We only know that they probably belonged to another ethnic family than the Greeks of classical times and that they took advantage of their excellent half-way position between Europe, Asia and Africa, in the heart of the Eastern Mediterranean, to build their power on maritime trade. In the thousand years between 2400 and 1400 BC the first great civilization ever to arise on European soil flowered in Crete, and particularly at Knossos. We will try to define it more fully when visiting Crete, the scene of its birth. It was brilliant and refined, favouring comfort and elegance. It disappeared irrevocably in a catastrophe in which the Achaean invaders from the Peloponnese played more than a minor role. With the Cretan people dead, the Greeks took the stage.

They entered Greece in the fifteenth century BC, great warriors from the north carrying bronze weapons and sporting moustaches and beards. They were the Achaeans, the ancestors of the heroes who fought for Helen before the walls of Troy. They do not represent the whole of the Greek people, but one of the families to which the Dorians were later joined, not without force, to form the Hellenic community of classical times. Under the Achaeans, the first really Greek civilization developed brilliantly, particularly in the plain of Argolis, at Mycenae 'rich in gold' (and archaeological discoveries have proved that a Homeric epithet has never been more justified). From acropolises bounded by gigantic ramparts, the kings of Mycenae, Tiryns, Pylos and Ithaca, installed in their comfortable palaces, administered their domains, inscribing their accounts on clay tablets which can now be deciphered. As sailors and warriors they increased their revenues by lucrative raids in fast boats, roved the seas or peacefully exchanged their painted pottery, filled with oil or wine, for gold and ivory from the East. The war with Troy is the last brilliant episode in their history. The bronze age ended. The Dorians, with weapons of iron, overcame Greece at the end of the twelfth century BC and plunged the country into confusion. Promise of a renaissance could, nevertheless, be discerned. The 'geometric' style succeeded the 'Mycenaean'. From the tenth to the eighth centuries the beautiful vases of Athens and Argos revealed the quality of severity and the sense of form which remain characteristic of Greek genius.

Under pressure from the Dorians the Achaeans installed themselves in the islands and on the coast of Asia Minor (where they were soon followed by the Dorians), taking with them their traditions. A major event had occurred: Hellenism had spread beyond the frontiers of little Greece. This Ionian coast saw a reflowering of letters and art—the epic with Homer of Chios, lyricism with Alcaeus and Sappho of Lesbos—while in the great coastal cities, Smyrna, Phocaea, Ephesus, Miletus, Clazomenos, the thinkers laid the foundations of science and western philosophy. This thin fringe of Hellenism resisted pressure from Persian, Arab and Turkish power for thirty centuries. The Treaty of

Lausanne suppressed it with one stroke of the pen after the Greek-Turkish war of 1923.

The moving frontiers of Greece were again extended during the period from the eighth to the sixth century BC, enlarging her intellectual horizon as well as her economic domain. It was the process known as colonization. The difficulty of feeding too large a population on too poor a soil and the social troubles which ensued forced the Greeks to seek their fortune on a more favoured land. Preferring adventure to hardship, a band of starvelings and political victims set sail one day, after praying to the god of Delphi to guide them to new countries. They founded cities on the coasts of the Black Sea, Africa, Sicily, Italy, Gaul and Spain in the image of those they had been forced to leave. Sybaris, Taranto, Syracuse, Selinos and Gela, Nice, Antibes, Marseilles, Ampurias in Spain, Cyrene in Africa and an obscure colony of Megara with a great future—Byzantium—were founded in this way. The Mediterranean became a Greek sea. One of the most original characteristics of ancient Greece was already evident: her dispersion in space. Greece is not a nation; she is a spiritual community very strongly bound together despite differences in temperament, dialect and institutions, a community reinforced and made real by the fundamental unity of language and religion. When the cities met at Delphi or Olympus in the great pan-Hellenic sanctuaries, to worship the same gods or compete in fraternal competitions, despite their jealousies and their quarrels, they understood that they were part of the same people, in the highest sense of the term. Yet at the same time they retained the independence so dear to them that they would die rather than renounce it.

Today we can scarcely imagine how original, even unique, the Greek ideal of the city as a community of free and equal individuals seemed in contrast to the great empires of the time, Egypt or Persia. The Greek citizen was free because he was only subject to the laws of the city and not to the arbitrariness of another man, as were slaves or barbarian subjects of a king. All citizens had equal rights before the law. Such at least was the ideal that was sought throughout the revolutions, when power passed from the king to the aristocracy, then to a popular leader or 'tyrant' and then to the people themselves. Outside his city the citizen was nothing, but it was he alone who brought the city into existence. The value of the city depended on the worth of the citizens. In the assembly of the nation, at the council of the Elders, they contributed to decisions on its policy. The citizen was directly responsible for its prosperity and glory, and this responsibility was the foundation of the human dignity of the individual. The barbarian was an irresponsible subject and, as such, despised. It was the duty of the citizen to develop his physical and mental capacity to the maximum to bring greater glory to the city, a glory which would be reflected on its children.

It is necessary to remember this to understand the significance and the repercussions of the Medean wars on Greek history, that great conflict when the Greek cities faced the immense empire under first Darius and then Xerxes. Surrender to Persia would have transformed Greece into a peaceful and perhaps even prosperous satrapy. But it would also have involved the renunciation of the title to citizenship, which gave man his self-respect. He would no longer assume the moral responsibility for his destiny. To save this precious civilization already wonderfully developed in all realms of art and thought the Greeks were capable of anything, even of forgetting their internal quarrels. The troops of Darius were pushed back at Marathon by the Athenian hoplites in 490 BC; those of Xerxes, despite their victory at Thermopylae and the occupation of Athens, which was voluntarily abandoned by its inhabitants, were defeated at Salamis in 480 and at Plataea in 479 by the cities united as closely as the bodies of the three bronze serpents they consecrated under a golden tripod at Delphi to thank Apollo for the victory. The energy and patriotism of the citizens, inferior in numbers, had triumphed over innumerable troops marching under the menace of the whip. This was decisive proof to the world of the excellence of the civilization they had fought for. Athens found a poet amongst her hoplites to sing in immortal verse the victory of the Dorian lance over the Medean bow: Aeschylus composed his tragedy *The Persians* where the suffering of the conquered barbarians acknowledges the glory of the triumphant cities.

Or rather, the glory of one city. In this harsh test, Athens had emerged as the wisest and most audacious of the cities: she had even sacrificed her town and surrendered her Acropolis to the fire of the invaders. She duly received the greatest part of the success. Till then, the model city, the city *par excellence*, the incarnation of all virtues, had been Dorian Sparta, whipped into an ascetic military discipline. The Medean wars marked the promotion of Athens, which after that became identified with Hellenism itself, gave it its most beautiful appearance, and carried it at one blow to the culminating point in its history. The goddess reigning over the devastated Acropolis gave rise to a statesman, Pericles, an artist, Phidias, architects and poets. Money was abundant—supplied by the Persians and also from contributions by allies defended by Athens against the Persians. It was a providential disaster that the Acropolis was razed to the ground. The field was clear for genius. The great rocky plateau was ready to receive a new set of monuments. In a burst of exalted enthusiasm, the whole city strove for perfection. Her democracy was the most rational and dignified. Four poets, Aeschylus, Sophocles, Euripides and Aristophanes, created the finest tragedies and comedies. A historian, Thucydides, laid the foundations of modern history. Her architects erected buildings of unequalled purity. And Phidias carved grave and noble faces in marble or in ivory which represent the very face of the Athens of Pericles.

The fifth century BC was truly the zenith. Athenian democracy was very shortly afterwards overthrown by demagogy in the civil wars. These excesses have been hidden by the brilliance of her greatness. Even the death of Socrates, which should have brought disgrace, has added a sublime page to her history—and a Plato appeared to write it. The cities could not survive the jealous struggles which rent them throughout the fifth and fourth centuries BC, in pursuit of an imaginary supremacy—a distorted form of the spirit of competition which is the basis of the Greek character and the foundation of its success. The fifth century, the century of Pericles, was disfigured by the atrocious Peloponnesian war when Sparta and Athens, 'Dorians' and 'Ionians', confronted one another mercilessly from 431 to 404. This civil war ended in 404 with the naval battle of Aigos Potamos when Athens collapsed under the blows of the Spartans. It was an ephemeral triumph. Sparta might well consecrate the thirty-seven bronze statues of her gods and her victorious admirals at Delphi; Thebes was already rising up before her. Under the leadership of a great soldier, Epaminondas, the Thebans crushed the conquerors of yesterday in 371 at Leuctra and arrived on Spartan soil where the women had never before seen the smoke of an enemy camp. The following year saw the end of Epaminondas in the uncertain battle of Mantinea. It was a time of vain battle and useless death. When the passionate call of Demosthenes persuaded the depopulated cities that the real danger came from the north, from Macedonia, it was already too late. In 338 BC when the heavy Macedonian phalanx, skilfully manœuvred by Philip, crushed Athens and Thebes in the plain of Chaeronea, the two opponents were finally reconciled. It was the victory of an organized realm over the absence of discipline so dear to the cities. Greek history had turned a page. Born in the city, Greek civilization had too great a human value to adapt itself to such narrow limits. The roots of the plant had burst the vase. It had to be transplanted to open country. This was the task undertaken by Alexander, the son of Philip. Once assured of authority in Greece, he departed to conquer Persia. Was this to revenge the Medean wars? One might have thought so. But what a difference between the state of mind of an Athenian hoplite fighting the 'barbarian' in 480 BC and this conqueror with his universal outlook, a disciple of Aristotle, who set out to understand the civilization of the enemy in order to enrich his own and thereby lay the foundations of a large human community beyond differences of race and religion. Symbolically, he married his officers to Persian wives and set the example himself by marrying Roxana, the daughter of Darius. Alexander and his forces led an amazing procession through Asia Minor to Phoenicia, Palestine and Egypt, to the heart of Babylon, from Bactria and Persia. He reached India and died in Babylon in 323 BC at the age of thirty-two, leaving a flashing path through history and having so successfully upset the old particularism of the Greeks that Hellenism, stretching to the frontiers of the known world, fully deserved to be called humanism.

The death of Alexander marked the beginning of what is conventionally known as the Hellenist epoch. The old cities still existed. They deliberated, issued decrees, minted money. But they were swayed by policies which they no longer controlled and their institutions ran in neutral gear. Power belonged henceforth to realms, organized and administered like modern states, into which Alexander's successors divided his immense empire, in Macedonia, Syria, Egypt. The Greek dynasty of the Ptolemies of which Cleopatra was the last queen installed themselves at Alexandria. The political equality, the source of pride of every citizen, was well and truly dead. As in the barbarian monarchies of the East, the Greek sovereign claimed divine honours and the Athenians lowered themselves to the extent of placing Demetrius Poliorcetis and his courtesans in the Parthenon.

The successors of Alexander, Antigonides, Seleucids, Ptolemies, destroyed themselves in useless battles as had the cities before them. And, as before, the wretched political situation did not prevent Greek civilization from extending its boundaries and progressing. Although Athens always shone with uncontested glory, although she remained (albeit deprived of political supremacy) the school of Greece, the sciences and arts flowered in new capitals: Alexandria, Pergamum, Antioch and Rhodes, where the bronze Colossus, a hundred feet high, was one of the seven wonders of the world. Greek humanism grew more profound. Down the centuries, the Greek had only conceived his philosophy and his morality within the solid framework of the city. Plato himself in *The Republic* drew up the plans for the ideal city. Suddenly this framework collapsed: man was obliged to revise his code of values, to seek support only in himself. Thus new philosophies of stoicism and scepticism were born. Human dignity and freedom were no longer based on the power of a common city but only on personal merit, regardless of external conditions of race or social status. Epictetus was a slave and Pyrrho a gardener. Art itself became more concerned with the peculiarities of the individual: the realistic portrait entered the picture. The picturesque was preferred to the abstract beauty of classicism—a triumph for the Alexandrian school of artists, and pathos—a triumph for the sculptors of Pergamum, or the theatrical—a triumph for those of Rhodes.

Often described as a time of decadence, the Hellenistic period was exceptionally brilliant in the field of science. When he founded the famous library at Alexandria, Ptolemy, son of Lagos, created the first modern institute of scientific research in Egypt. One of its directors, Aristophanes of Byzantium, published critical editions of the great ancient authors and the knowledge that we have of them rests to a large extent on his scholarly work. Eratosthenes of Cyrene, another director of the library, established a rational historical chronology and calculated the length of the terrestrial circumference with amazing precision. Aristarchus of Samos, eighteen centuries before Copernicus, proclaimed that the earth revolved round the sun. In mathematics, Euclid published his *Elements of Geometry*. Archimedes laid the foundations of modern physics.

And in the *Treatise on Machines* by the engineer Hero of Alexandria there is the first model of a steam turbine ever conceived in the world. The author was far from suspecting its practical utility in a country without fuel and where slaves were so cheap.

The Greeks of the Hellenistic period were therefore not decadent. But they were divided, as if by the past, worn out by an almost continual state of war. Exploiting these rivalries, the Roman Senate, by skilful and tenacious policies, easily absorbed Greece into its empire. Rome first clashed with the powerful realm of Macedonia. The consul Flaminius fought Philip V at Cynocephalus in 197 BC and 'liberated' Greece from Macedonian protection. He solemnly proclaimed this liberty at the Isthmic Games in 196 and annexed Macedonia, the first strip of Hellenism to become a Roman province. But the Greeks were becoming restless. The year of the destruction of Carthage in 146, the consul Mummius brutally checked the rebellion of the Achaean League and razed Corinth. The territory of that antique and glorious city remained abandoned until the foundation of the Augustan colony which re-created it at the beginning of the present era. Under Augustus, Greece became the province of Achaea, a vast museum drawn on by the emperors to decorate their palaces. But in Rome, Hellenism was absorbed into the spirit of its conquerors. The century of Augustus was nourished on the century of Pericles. Hellenism first passed into Latin culture from Rome, before the Renaissance drew it directly from its source.

Absorbed into the Roman Empire, Greece detached herself from it in the form of a Greek empire almost as large as that of Alexander, which survived for a thousand years: the Byzantine Empire. In order to resist barbarian attacks on the over-long frontiers of the Roman world, Diocletian and Constantine at the beginning of the fourth century decided to share the power between two 'Caesars' and two 'Augustuses' who would govern and defend the empire divided into two zones, one western and the other eastern. The system was known as the tetrarchy. Constantine, one of the tetrarchs, rapidly eliminated the three others and decided to establish his capital on a site nearer the frontiers and better situated than Rome on the great trading routes. In 324 he chose the site of Byzantium, the old Megarian colony, where he built Constantinople, the town of Constantine. After immense raids on Greek sanctuaries, he was able to give it the artistic appearance it lacked. Surrounded with walls, the city was filled with basilicas and palaces. The decadence of Rome and the barbarian invasion of the Western Empire made the Eastern Empire the real representative of Rome. Constantine, although he was rightly regarded by the Greeks as the founder of the Byzantine Empire, and although the Orthodox Church had inscribed him in the ranks of its saints, like his successors, like Justinian who exhausted himself in the sixth century trying to reconquer the Western Empire from the barbarians, considered himself the head of the Roman Empire. The century of Justinian was a golden century in the realm of art, letters and law. Pericles erected the Parthenon; Justinian constructed St Sophia, the most beautiful dwelling offered to God since the temple of Solomon.

Meanwhile Byzantium became increasingly conscious of her true character: where she faced the Latins, she was a Grecian empire; facing the Slavs, the Arabs, the Bulgars and the Ottomans, a Christian one. During this epoch the Greek Orthodox religion became the very expression of national sentiment. The splendour of Byzantium, as opposed to the decadence of Rome, favoured the development of the Church of the East, for a long time the most active and the most prosperous. The great councils of the church were held in the Orient, at Ephesus, Antioch and Nicaea.

In this brilliant period, Greece proper, except in rare cases, only played a secondary part. The empire was wearing itself out fighting unceasingly against the ever-rising sea of barbarian invasions. The bastion of Christianity, it staggered paradoxically under the blows of Christian nations—the commercial interests of Venice, the jealousies of Rome and the forces of religious hatred which sent the ships of the Crusades against Constantinople. It was a tragedy for the civilized world when the town was taken in 1204. The art treasures and precious manuscripts were pillaged or burnt. The empire was divided amongst the Latins. For a time French dukes reigned over Athens and Argos and in Salonika troubadours from Provence sang of courtly love. The Peloponnese bristled with the castles of the Franks; the Lord of Villehardouin held his court at Mistra. Despite a late Byzantine renaissance, Constantinople, reconquered by the Greeks, easily succumbed to a Turkish attack in 1453. There ended the Byzantine Empire.

As a province of the Ottoman Empire, Greece vegetated and slept. The great towns of yore with their evocative names—Athens, Corinth, Argos— slowly became miserable villages ravaged by malaria, amidst the ruins of ancient monuments where travellers came to dream and philosophize. A minaret grew up on the Parthenon. A harem arose behind the virginal caryatids of the Erechtheum. The church alone kept national sentiment alive. That it was still alive was shown in the nineteenth century by the open revolt against Ottoman power. In 1821, the epic of the revolution began in the Peloponnese, bringing to the fore those picturesque heroes with large moustaches and red caps, armed with silver pistols, whose names resound like rifle fire: Theodoros Kolokotronis, Dikeos Papaflessas, Karaiskakis, Admiral Miaoulis. The sympathy of liberal Europe with the cause of Greek independence and the need to maintain their influence in the East led Russia, France and England to impose an armistice on the belligerents. When the Porte refused to submit to this, a fleet sent by the Triple Alliance annihilated the Turko-Egyptian fleet in the Bay of Navarino where formerly the palace of old Nestor stood, in 1827. In 1832, Turkey officially recognized Greek independence, together with the monarch chosen by the three powers: Otho the First, Prince of Bavaria. Greece, her territory reduced to the Peloponnese, the Cyclades and the south of Thessaly, patiently set to work to reconquer the whole of her dominion: Thessaly and the district of Arta in 1881; Crete, recognized as 'autonomous' by Turkey in 1897. As a result of the Balkan wars in 1912 and 1913, she almost attained the frontiers which are hers today. On November 8, 1912, Salonika was occupied by Greek troops and also Mount Athos. The Treaty of Bucarest in 1913 brought the frontier back to the Nestos and established the link between Crete and the archipelago of Greece. The 'catastrophe' of Asia Minor drove Greece from the Ionian coast where the Achaeans had established themselves ten centuries before Christ. The Treaty of Lausanne in 1923 brutally but radically removed all problems by decreeing the obligatory exchange of minorities between Greece, Bulgaria and Turkey. The Jewish community at Salonika was almost entirely massacred during the German occupation of 1940–1944, so thoroughly that today with eight million inhabitants there are only Greeks in Greece, except for the Turkish minorities in the Dodecanese and a community of eighty thousand Turks allowed to live in eastern Macedonia in exchange for the retention of eighty thousand Greeks at Istanbul. The Dodecanese was returned to Greece in 1947, as a just recompense for the courage which inflicted the first great defeat on Axis troops during the last world war, in the mountains of Epirus. The co-existence of a Turkish community and a much larger Greek community in the large island of Cyprus raises a problem which the granting of independence to the island in 1959 has not solved.

*
* *

When Greece was cut off from Europe which she had civilized and was no longer anything but a poor nation of peasants and sailors, travellers often asked if the Greeks they met were really the descendants of the Greeks of olden times. Would Pericles recognize as a compatriot the Athenian bourgeois with his black hair, and slightly corpulent, discussing politics with the help of wide gestures over his cup of coffee and his glass of fresh water? The shaven *loustro* whose brushes fly briskly over our shoes? The village priest wearing a blue blouse, tossing along on his ass as he goes to prune his vine, dragging his goat along at the end of its tether? Have not four centuries of Ottoman domination dissolved the occupant and the occupier into one bastard race? This has not been the case because religion has always erected a hard and fast barrier between the Orthodox and the Moslem. Greece has preserved her integrity by those strong family traditions which even today prevent, for example, the eldest brother from marrying until he has established and endowed his sisters. Finally the Greek language effectively helped to safeguard national solidarity. Despite the inevitable changes which affect all living languages, modern Greek is directly descended from the language spoken by the rulers of Mycenae, by Demosthenes and Plato. It is no less ridiculous to search amongst the Greeks for a true Dorian or a pure Achaean than amongst the French for a Salian Frank or an authentic Arverne. Since the dawn of her history, too rich in humanity to confine herself strictly to one race, Hellenism has expanded and intermingled. Eumenes, the Phocaean landing at Marseilles, married the Gallic princess who handed him the cup of hydromel. At Thasos, Greek colonists of Paros and native Thracians mingled within the walls of the same city. As in all western countries, the disruption caused by successive invasions has made the idea of race obsolete in Greece but has left intact the much richer conception of a people. More than a race, more than a nation, the Greeks are a people. The face of the people changes because the face is alive. Without ever being exactly the same it is never entirely different and the alterations introduced by history never eliminate the permanent fundamentals.

The most striking trait of the Greek character, and that which makes for the most agreeable and easy relationships, is certainly the profound sense of human equality inherited directly from the classical *polis*. Differences of situation or fortune never prevent a Greek from feeling himself the equal as a human being of any other Greek or of any other man, whoever he may be. Success and wealth are considered the result of *savoir faire;* they signify intelligence, astuteness or luck and the rich would no more dream of concealing their richness than the poor of being annoyed by it even if they envy it. A Greek peasant is perfectly at ease with a minister; a minister is not self-conscious with a peasant. They are two similar men placed differently by destiny. Unless they have been specifically ordered to show 'outward signs of respect' workmen on an excavation site will spontaneously address the archaeologist in familiar terms and call him by his Christian name and do so without misplaced familiarity, as one man to another, taking it for granted that you should speak to them in the same way. There is no servility: in the poorest areas of the country they never beg, they always offer. Poverty has diminished neither their pride nor their self-respect. The poorest man has always a few drachmae in his pocket on a Saturday to have his beard shaved and his shoes polished. And on a Sunday, seeing the flirtatious crowd coming and going on the *platia* (the central square of the town or village), boys to one side, girls to the other, one would never suspect that for more than one of them, tomorrow's bread is still a problem to be solved.

The Greek is the most sociable man there is. His happiness is not complete unless he can enjoy it surrounded by a beautiful *parea*, that is to say in a large crowd. He strikes up acquaintanceships far more easily because he is not hampered by superfluous etiquette. He questions you immediately about your native land, your wife, the number of your children, the size of your income. It would be wrong to regard these signs of interest as indiscreet. He will tell you about himself with the same simplicity. He will ask, without waiting, your opinion of his country, which he loves passionately but without xenophobia; he will cut himself in half to help you out of difficulty and will offer you his house if you need accommodation, even if he himself has to sleep in the open air with his wife and children as a result. It is banal to praise Greek hospitality; not to mention it would be ungrateful. His taste for society, his curiosity of mind, his personal pride, the love of his country and without doubt an old and deeply rooted tradition unite to make the Greek a hospitable being. Whether ostentatious or restrained this hospitality always represents the most he is able to afford.

We visited Chios after an earth tremor had affected many villages on the island. On the ramparts of the Genoese *castro* we met an old woman who had taken refuge in a tower after her house had been destroyed; she had saved a pot of basil in a tin can. She questioned us on our origins and told us her misfortunes. Then she took the trouble to go down to the fountain so that the water she offered us to accompany the *glyko* should be really fresh. When we left, she cut us two branches of her basil and wished us luck with true warmth. We were totally unknown to her. It is these beautiful human qualities which bind the Greek people most closely to their ancestors of olden times and which give visitors to Greece additional reason to love her.

This portrait of the Greek people would be incomplete without some mention of their religious convictions. The small icons hung in motor coaches and taxis, perpetually lit by a small red bulb, the numerous chapels scattered along the roadsides where the traveller crosses himself in passing, the over-ambitious and often unfinished churches whose domes overlook the houses of the poorest villages, all quite clearly indicate that the Greeks are a pious people. The Christian religion is intimately associated in their memory with the splendours of the Byzantine Empire, and in the darkest moments of its history the church remained the sole force of cohesion and national unity. To claim that one was Orthodox was a way of claiming that one was Greek, as opposed to Moslem, or Latin and western Papist incarnate in the conquering Crusader or the mercantile Venetian. Even today, there is still a certain fusion between religion and the expression of patriotism, which makes the position of the small Catholic communities existing in the heart of the Greek nation morally delicate, despite the broad spirit of tolerance which animates the nation.

The distance between Orthodoxy and Roman Catholicism is in fact very small. They are not divorced but physically separated. There is no reciprocal accusation of heresy, simply a *schism* (a fissure) more administrative, it might be said, than religious. The Orthodox Church believes that the Holy Ghost proceeds from the Father but not from the Son. It does not admit the dogma of the Immaculate Conception and tolerates the marriage of priests under certain conditions. The theological divergences invoked by the two churches were rather religious pretexts to cover more temporal causes: political rivalries, the perpetual quarrels over precedence between Rome and Byzantium, equally armed with proud pretensions to the title of capital of the empire and of Christianity. In the eleventh century, after mutual excommunications, the schism was consummated. As a result of this, the Orthodox churches do not recognize the supreme authority of the Pope but are 'autocephalous', each submitting to its own patriarch: the Russian Church to the Patriarch of Moscow, the Church of Cyprus to Nicosia, the Coptic Church to Alexandria, and, finally, the Greek Church to the Patriarch of Constantinople.

The Greek people regard their clergy with a feeling of respect mingled with irreverence, not dissimilar to that of the French in the Middle Ages, whose deep faith was mixed with a type of permanent anticlericalism. Respected for his sacerdotal functions, the village priest does not always escape mockery from his parishioners. He is close to them in his poverty as in his virtues, and also often in the crude everyday problems which the father of a family must solve—because he has the right to marry. But in a land where 'to earn one's bread by the sweat of one's brow' is not simply a rhetorical image, his position, however modest, as a government-paid official, may give rise to envy. He is the object—sometimes the irritated victim—of strange superstitions: for example, it is considered an evil omen to meet the priest in the morning in the street when leaving the house. We have seen the driver of a motor bus, though a very worthy man and pious towards the icons on his dashboard, leave an unfortunate village *papas*, surrounded by his baskets, by the roadside in the early morning. Ill luck had decreed that he should be the first traveller to be waiting at the first stop!

Like all Mediterranean Christian nations, the Greeks offer particularly fervent devotion to the Virgin—the *Panaghia*, that is to say the All-Holy. Every year, the Marian festivals are the occasion for magnificent processions, particularly on the island of Tinos. These festivals, as well as Christmas and Easter, give excellent opportunities to admire the display of the Orthodox liturgy, which perpetuates the imperial splendours of Byzantium in the middle of the twentieth century and the beautiful employment of a form of sacred music in which the human voice is considered the only instrument worthy of singing the praises of the Creator.

A minimal knowledge of the history of Greek art is required if you desire to profit fully from a trip to Greece. Too great an ignorance would leave you confused before the profusion of wonders. What follows is not meant to replace personal study. Its object is merely to give a sort of systematic guide, necessary to facilitate comprehension of this book.

When we visit Crete and Argolis, we shall describe the brilliant civilization

which the Cretans and Mycenaeans created in the eastern basin of the Mediterranean and which lasted over two thousand years. It was ruined by the Dorian
invasion: an obscure period which saw the birth and development of the style
known as 'geometric'. From the tenth to the eighth centuries BC, artists used
simple combinations of straight lines and curves for their designs and reduced
the representation of living things, men and animals, painted on vases, modelled
in clay or cast in bronze, to schemes which were elementary but not rudi-
mentary. The simple media did not exclude life, or force, or grace from the
work. The masterpieces of this period are the great funeral vases of the Dipylon,
thrown by Attic potters, and the rich collection of vases excavated at Argos
by the French School of Athens, the products of local industry and an expression
of original taste which can now be admired at the new museum in the town.
The evolution towards a less abstract and more life-like representation than
that found in the geometric style was hastened by repeated contacts between
the Greeks and the East. In the seventh century BC new motifs appeared in
the Greek style, inspired by the curios which Phoenician and Cypriot merchants
were spreading on the banks of the Aegean Sea. This 'oriental' period is
marked by the representation of familiar animals in an exotic and fabulous
manner, ranged in long lines, or heraldically as on a coat of arms: deer, bulls,
birds, lions, sphinxes and griffins, beaten on bronze leaves, carved on ivory
slabs or painted on the sides of the beautiful vases of Rhodes, Athens and
Corinth.

The sixth century BC was exceptionally rich in all realms of art. For
religious purposes the gods were represented in human form; the worshipper
was urged to demonstrate his piety by consecrating an effigy, representing
sometimes the god, sometimes the worshipper himself, but always in the
highly symbolic, impersonal form of a glorious body, all harmony, vigour
and youth. The sanctuaries thus favoured the flowering of that great sculpture
at which the Greeks soon became masters. There was the *couros*, the young
athlete, in the nudity of the stadium, with broad shoulders, narrow hips, his
arms at his sides unless his hand held some offering, his left foot forward and
a smile on his lips. And his sister, the *core*, the young girl in a Dorian *peplos* or
a long Ionian tunic covered by a skilfully draped cloak. They are in marble,
painted in bright colours, in bronze, or sometimes in ivory and gold like the
statues of Apollo, Artemis and Leto found at Delphi under the Sacred Way.
Although at first they were always shown upright and full face, these two
types, the *couros* and the *core*, repeated over and over again, finished by becoming
more supple. Architecture played a certain part in this evolution, as the need
for fixing statues in the pediments of temples obliged artists to fold them into
complicated positions—lying down, crouching—to decorate the corners of
the triangular frame. Thus Greek art broke free from the rigid law of frontal
positions, which Egyptian art, for example, only achieved on rare occasions.

Architecture also produced masterpieces from the very beginning. They were born from the happy union of a spirit endowed with the ability to feel and to express the difficult beauties of the most abstract harmonies in combination with the geological resources of a land rich in exceptionally high-quality quarries: the Peloponnese, particularly Corinth and Sicyon and the peninsula of the Piraeus in Attica, supply the tender limestone, the *poros*, used to build almost all the temples in the Peloponnese as well as the archaic temples of Athens. A royal material, white marble sparkles on the flanks of Mounts Hymettus and Pentelicon and on most of the islands, Thasos, Naxos and Paros. Severe and pure taste at first prevented the use of tinted or veined marbles—blue marble from Tinos, mottled marble from Scyros, speckled stone from Croceai in Loconia—which Roman and Byzantine architects, on the other hand, later used intemperately. However, from the archaic period, dark-blue limestone from Eleusis and black stone from Argos were coupled with white marble to obtain very discreet polychrome effects. The various parts which make up a Greek building, fitted with extreme precision, are bonded with sharp joints, by simple juxtaposition without the use of mortar, though sometimes joined together by iron clamps and gudgeons fixed in with lead. The buildings were enhanced with colours which emphasized their constituent elements: the base with its steps, and the columns of the temple, remained white; the architrave was also white but was edged at the top, in the Doric order, by a thin red band in relief, the *tenia*, emphasized at the plumb of the triglyphs by blue *regulae*. The triglyphs of the frieze were blue; the metopes, flat or sculptured with reliefs, were also coloured; the weather-mouldings were blue and red, and decorated, like the sloping gutters, with palm leaves. The statues of the fronton, which were also painted, stood out against the blue background of the tympanums. The mouldings which effected the transition between the various sections of the temple and which have formed the basis of the decorative repertoire of western architecture right up to modern times—crow's beak, talon, cyma, ovolo, astragal—were decorated with delicate motifs, sculptured or painted: water-leaves, ogees, beads and pirouettes. The beauty of the stone, the severe harmony of the proportions, the gaiety of the colour and the delicacy of the profile make this architecture one of the purest achievements of the Greek genius.

As with sculpture, religion, above all else, attracted the genius of the architects: the Ionic style is illustrated in the giant temples of Artemis at Ephesus, of Hera at Samos, and at Delphi in the four miniature masterpieces, which are the four marble chapels or 'treasuries' of Knidos, Siphnos, Marseilles and the 'anonymous one'. Meanwhile the Doric order wavered between the slender proportions of the first temple of Athena at Delphi, with columns as thin as posts, and the thick-set proportions of the temple of Apollo at Corinth with thick monolithic columns. It then succeeded in reconciling vigour with

3

Egine. Le temple
Athéna Aphaia.

3. Aegina. The Temple of
Athena Aphaia.

3. Tempel in Ägina.

4

5

6

4-5-6. Au Pirée.　　　　4-5-6. At the Piraeus.　　　　4-5-6. Im Hafen von Pirä

7

Athènes et le Lycabette
de l'Acropole.

7. Athens and Lycabettos
seen from the Acropolis.

7. Blick von der Akropolis auf
Athen und den Lycabettos.

8

8-9-10. *Aspects de la vie en Grèce.*

8-9-10. *Aspects*

reek life.

8-9-10. Szenen aus dem Leben der Griechen.

11

11. *Entre Corinthe et*
le lac de Vouliagméni.

11. *Between Corinth and*
Lake Vouliagmeni.

11. *In der Nähe von Korint*

12

13

. Lycéens d'Andritsaina.   12. Schoolboys from Andritsaina.   12. Schüler von Andritsaina.

. A Epidaure.   13. At Epidaurus.   13. In Epidaurus.

14

15

18

19

16

14-15-16-17. Art des Cyclades.
Le harpiste (14), le flûtiste (15),
tête (16), statue féminine (17).
18. Personnage ithyphallique assis.
Thessalie. Néolithique récent.
19. Mycènes. Tête en Calcaire.

14-15-16-17. Art of the Cyclades.
The Harpist (14). The Flautist (15).
Head (16). Female figure (17).
18. Seated figure from Thessalia.
Late neolithic.
19. Mycenae: limestone head.

14-15-16-17. Kunst von den Zykladen.
Der Harfenist (14). Der Flötist (15).
Kopf (16). Weibliche Figur (17).
18. Sitzende Gestalt aus Thessalien.
Spätes Neolithikum.
19. Mykene. Kopf aus Kalkstein.

17

Athens.

Nationalmuseum Athen.

Musée d'Héracleion.
20-21-22.
Idoles crétoises.
Musée National
d'Athènes.
23. Joueur de flûte
de Samos.

20

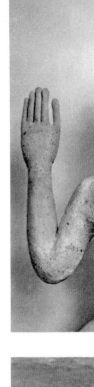

Museum of Heraklion.
20-21-22.
Cretan idols.
National Museum of
Athens.
23. Flute player from Samos.

Museum von Heraklion.
20-21-22.
Kretische Idole.
Nationalmuseum Athen.
23. Der Flötenspieler
von Samos.

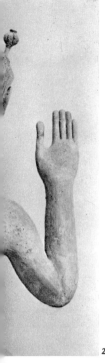

21

22

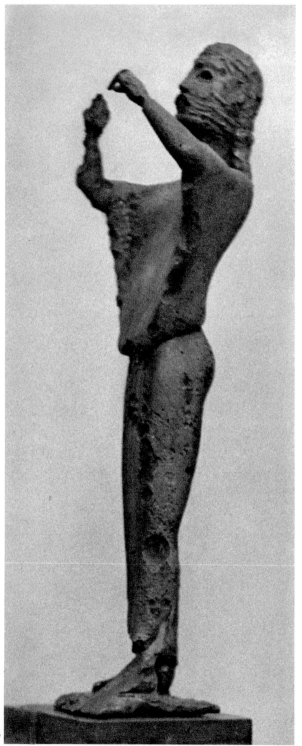

23

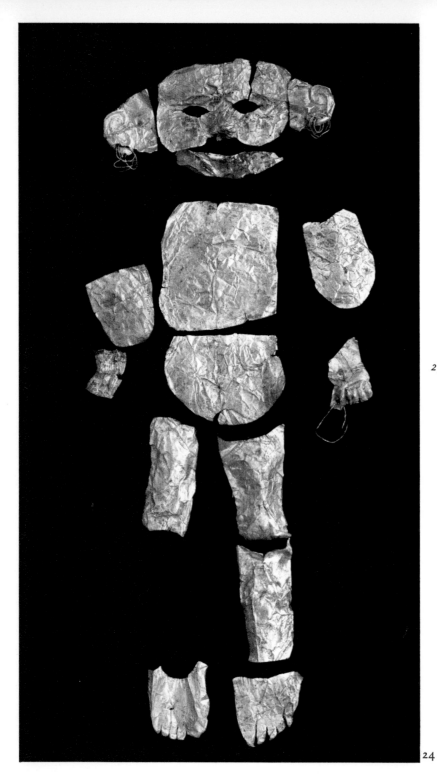

26

27

28

29

30

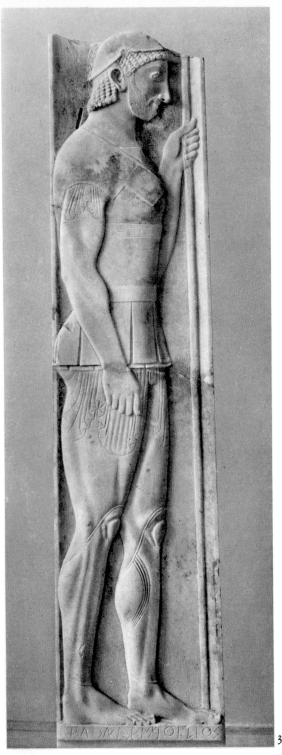

31

34

35

Musée National d'Athènes.
35. Bas-relief d'Eleusis.

National Museum of Athens.
35. Bas-relief from Eleusis.

Nationalmuseum Athen.
35. Relief in Eleu.

36

sée National d'Athènes.   *National Museum of Athens.*   *Nationalmuseum Athen.*
Stèle de l'hoplitodrome.   *36. Stele from the hoplitodrom.*   *36. Grabstele von Hoplitodrom.*

37-38-39. Corés du musée de l'Acropole.

37-38-39. Core from

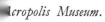

Acropolis Museum.　　　　　　　　　*37-38-39. Koren im Akropolis-Museum.*

*Musée National
d'Athènes.*

*40. Couros de
Volomandra.*

41. Couros de Milo.

42. Couros d'Anavyssos.

*National Museum
of Athens.*

40. Couros of Volomandra.

41. Couros of Milo.

42. Couros of Anavyssos.

*Nationalmuseum
Athen.*

*40. Kouros von
Volomandra.*

41. Kouros von Milo.

42. Kouros von Anavyssos.

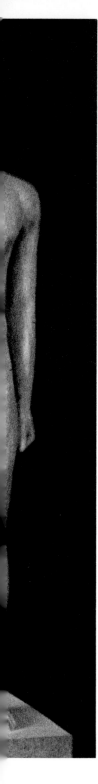

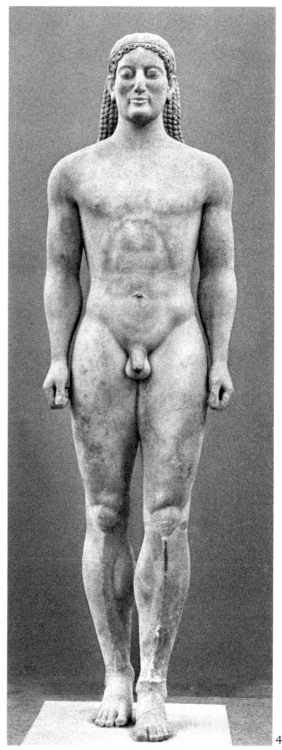

41

42

43

Musée National d'Athènes.   National Museum of Athens.   Nationalmuseum Athen.

43. L'Ephèbe de Marathon.   43. Ephebe from Marathon.   43. Ephebe aus Marath

44

usée National d'Athènes.   National Museum of Athens.   Nationalmuseum Athen.

. L'Ephèbe d'Anticythère.   44. Ephebe from Anticythera.   44. Ephebe aus Antikythera.

Musée National d'Athènes.

45. Bijoux d'or mycéniens.

46. Couronne de laurier en or (époque hellénistique).

47. Médaillon orné d'un buste d'Aphrodite (époque hellénistique)

48. Bracelets à tête de serpent (époque hellénistique).

National Museum of Athens.

45. Mycenaean gold jewellery.

46. Laurel crown in gold (Hellenistic period).

47. Medallion decorated with a bust of Aphrodite (Hellenistic period).

48. Bracelets with serpents' head (Hellenistic period).

45

46

Nationalmuseum Athen.

45. Goldschmuck aus Mykene.

46. Lorbeerkranz aus Gold (Hellenistische Epoche).

47. Medaillon mit Büste der Aphrodite (Hellenistische Epoche).

48. Armreifen mit Schlangenköpfen (Hellenistische Epoche).

47

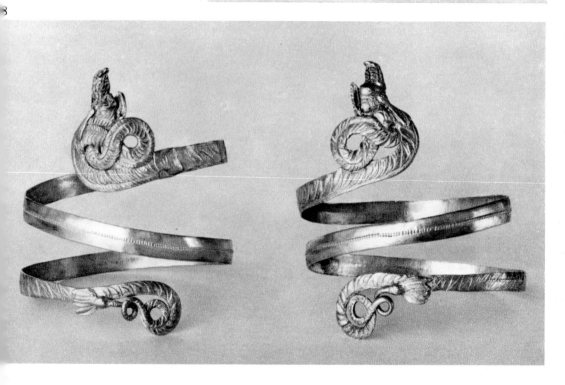

49

49. *Athènes. Musée Byzantin.*
Orphée.

49. *Athens. Byzantine Museum.*
Orpheus.

49. *Athen. Byzantinisches Muse*
Orpheus.

elegance in the constructions of the second half of the century. While Pisistratus and his son erected or embellished the Hecatompedon, or 'temple of a hundred feet', on the Acropolis, their political rivals, the Alcmeonides, erected a new temple of Apollo at Delphi, with frontons decorated by the great sculptor Antenor. The prosperous cities of Magna Graecia and Sicily, Posidonia (Paestum), Syracuse, Agrigentum, Selinus, by mingling Doric and Ionic influences, succeeded in creating an original style.

In sculpture as in architecture, Athenian artists again in the second half of the sixth century found equals or masters in Asia Minor, the islands and the Peloponnese. But in the realm of ceramics they were indisputably superior. While Corinthian pottery weakened and disappeared under competition, the Attic ceramists flooded the Mediterranean basin with vases decorated with scenes taken from mythology or family life. This living illustration of history, of incalculable value to historians, comprises real masterpieces, sometimes signed by their authors. The painter designed the silhouettes of his figures on a red base of natural clay with black varnish. Then he inscribed details of anatomy and dress, cutting the varnish with a dry point. The technique used on these vases with black figures was characteristic of archaic ceramics. However, during the last quarter of the sixth century a new and more subtle technique appeared: that of the vases with red figures. The artist painted the vase black, retaining the silhouette of the characters in the red colour of the clay. The details were then painted with a very fine brush in black varnish. After Amasis and Exekias, masters of the black-figure style, potters such as Andokides and Nicosthenes illustrate the period of transition which paved the way for the great flowering of the fifth century.

The Medean wars marked the end of the archaic period, and inaugurated 'classicism' which blossomed out during the fifth and fourth centuries BC. The victory over the Medes confirmed Greek self-confidence, and carried her along on a veritable wave of creation: Athena on the island of Aegina, Poseidon on the Isthmus and Zeus at Olympia were endowed with new temples in *poros*, decorated with marble sculptures. Athens decked itself in marble, reconstructed its Acropolis and its devastated *agora*. The first half of the century saw the advance of Greek genius towards perfection. In Attic red-figure ceramics, the 'severe style' of the great artists flowered. There was Epictetos, the painter who decorated bowls and plates with scenes borrowed from the life of the Ephebes, and from the banquets and revels of the Satyrs; Euphronios who drew his inspiration for preference from scenes from the life of Hercules; Douris; and Brygos, the epic painter, a genius equal to Euphronios. In sculpture, at the same period, sculptors blossomed of whom almost nothing but their names is known, but whom the ancient peoples numbered amongst the greatest. Pythagoras of Rhegium (possibly sculptor of the charioteer at Delphi), Calamis (possibly sculptor of the great bronze Zeus in the National Museum at Athens),

C

Myron and his famous *Discus-Thrower*, Polycletus of Argos (creator of the 'canon' or golden rule for human proportions), heralded the divine era in Greek art which it was left to Phidias to perpetuate in marble, ivory and gold. After so much austere beauty, the second half of the century showed the need for relaxation: the sculptor and goldsmith Callimachus, the painter of vases, Meidias, were content with a preciousness full of grace, while on the Acropolis, the Winged Victories carved on the parapet of the Erechtheum, the temple to Athena Nike, enlivened the Olympian majesty of the Parthenon with their delicate architecture.

This tendency of the fifth century was accentuated during the fourth. The incessant wars, the criticism of traditional religion by the philosophers, shook the faith of Hellenism in its gods and in itself. Praxiteles carved the gods of a sensual and rejuvenated Olympia; ungainly Hermes and Apollos with equivocal charms, Aphrodites henceforth stripped of their veils. Lysippus gave his athletes long and flexible bodies; Scopas reflected, in the pathetic expressions of his characters and in the outburst of his frantic Bacchante, the unrest of a civilization whose traditional framework was collapsing. The fourth century saw the decay of Attic ceramics with red figures. The masterpieces of terra-cotta were no longer vases but exquisite statuettes modelled by the Boeotian artists of Tanagra.

Whereas Athens, ruined by war with Sparta, did not have the means to complete the Propylaea or the temple of Nemesis at Rhamnonte, there was a veritable blossoming of temples in the Peloponnese during the fourth century: a new temple to Hera near Argos, to Poseidon on the Isthmus, to Zeus at Nemea and to Athena at Tegaea. A complete sanctuary with temples, porticos, theatre and stadium rose at Epidaurus in honour of Aesculapius, or Asclepios, god of medecine. While remaining faithful to the teachings of the great Attic architecture of the fifth century, the architects yet avoided that complete submission which might have led to academicism; instead they plunged into the pathways of the future. The Corinthian order was henceforth added to the two fundamental orders, the Doric and the Ionic. The oldest Corinthian capital appeared in the temple of Bassae in Arcadia. It was invented, according to Vitruvius, in the fifth century BC by the Athenian sculptor Callimachus, but was favoured in the fourth century by the architects and contractors of Epidaurus, precisely those who also built the marble *tholos* at Delphi and the limestone temple to Athena, and the new temple to Apollo, the work of the Corinthian Spintharos. For these artists travelled: Timotheos the sculptor of the temple of Asclepios at Epidaurus, Scopus who reconstructed the temple of Athena at Tegaea, and Leochares to whom we may possibly owe the Philippeion of Olympia, were united in Caria to build the sumptuous tomb of King Mausolus, the Mausoleum of Halicarnassus, one of the wonders of the world. And this explains how, at this period, the Peloponnese with its Dorian tradition can be seen adopting the Ionic order, and the Doric order is found taking root in Ionia. Just as the Greeks of the fourth century rose above provincial particularism and adopted a common language, the *koiné*, which is only the Attic dialect brought to perfection, so Greek art tended more towards a sort of aesthetic *koiné*, a purified expression of its genius. For the first time in the world great stone circular theatres at Athens, Corinth, Argos, Epidaurus and soon all over Greece, replaced the simple wooden scaffoldings which had satisfied the contemporaries of Sophocles and Euripides.

The period which extends from the death of Alexander (323 BC) to the Roman conquest in the second century BC is called the 'Hellenistic' period, because pure Hellenism was enriched—others might say contaminated—by elements borrowed from oriental peoples. The essential characteristics have already been defined. In the great cosmopolitan cities of Pergamum, Ephesus, Miletus, Rhodes, Delos and Alexandria, the most diverse peoples—Egyptians, Syrians, Jews, Italians, Gauls—came into contact; ideas and religions interpenetrated and mingled in a confused syncretism. Art could scarcely help reflecting this movement of ideas. It was an eclectic epoch: the classicism of the Aphrodite of Milo stood next to the passion of the gods and giants fighting on the frieze of the great altar to Zeus at Pergamum, with the terrible pathos of the group of Laocoon, the victim of the serpent of Poseidon, the probable work of a Rhodian sculptor. Great painting developed; mosaic, in full flight, benefited from its progress: it is from this period that there originated the few marvels of mosaic found at Delos and Pompeii.

Roman art adopted the Hellenistic tradition and perfected it. However, the prestige of the fifth century and the taste of amateur art-collectors for classical work continued to support an academicism not always devoid of merit —for example the statue of Antinous, a favourite of Hadrian, at Delphi. The renaissance of Greek art supported by the philhellenic emperors, in particular Hadrian, was too artificial to have real significance.

The pagan gods were really dead and with them a certain ideal of beauty. But Greek genius found other means of expression in Christianity, by a new approach to art. The 'Byzantine' epoch began with the founding of Constantinople in the fourth century AD.

The cult of Christianity which united her worshippers inside a sacred edifice, the church, when pagans nearly always celebrated their ceremonies in front of the temple, around an open-air altar, necessitated the construction of great edifices. The basilica was borrowed from Hellenic architecture and the domed church, whose vast possibilities were to be boldly demonstrated by the two architects of St Sophia at Constantinople, Anthemios of Tralles and Isidore of Miletus, in the sixth century AD, was perfected. The art of mosaic reached its splendour: the unsurpassed display at Ravenna remains the most beautiful example of this art.

63

In the seventh century a dramatic dispute divided the Eastern Church: was it suitable to represent God and the saints materially and to render to these images a homage often very close to idolatry? Very happily for the future of Byzantine art, if not for the purity of the faith, the 'iconoclasts', the destroyers of images, were not able to overcome the superstitious customs of the people, wilfully encouraged by the monks who made substantial profits from trade in images and from the cult of miraculous icons. A triumph for the puritans would probably have deprived us of the mosaics of Daphni, the frescoes of Salonika and Mistra, in effect the collection of icons which compose the richness of the Byzantine Museum at Athens.

The Turkish conquest stifled the development of the arts in Greece. Yet until the eighteenth century, Crete maintained outside the Ottoman Empire, thanks to the Venetian occupation, a celebrated school of painters of icons. One day a young artist, impregnated with their traditions, abandoned his Cretan village to go and seek his fortune in Italy and Spain: Domenico Theotocopouli, El Greco.

I. ATHENS AND ATTICA

AN educated Westerner cannot conceive Greece with any capital but Athens. However, if the heroes of 1821 had been asked what town they would choose to govern the state they were liberating, doubtless very few would have dreamt of the miserable hamlet huddled at the foot of a ruined acropolis and dominated by a Venetian tower and a Turkish minaret. They would have turned to the *Polis*, the town *par excellence*, Constantinople. The modern name, Istanbul, a deformation of the Greek *eis ten Polin*—towards the town, remains a reminder of a visionary hope, of a *Grande Idée* which haunted generations and which was ruined in 1922 in the catastrophe of Asia Minor. They would have preferred the town of Constantine to that of Pericles! As a result of a spontaneous emotion—which classical education, however, is in process of modifying —the Greek people had for a long time felt more closely bound to the Christian empire of Byzantium than to distant antiquity. They certainly admire it and are proud of it, but in a completely intellectual way, because they can scarcely recognize the image of their own nation in the ancient multitude of cities.

To designate Athens as capital, in the absence at the time of any more developed town, was the idea of a professor or an archaeologist which experience has proved to be sound. In 1834, Athens numbered three hundred houses. Today, with Piraeus, it shelters 1,800,000 inhabitants. This simple comparison explains the phenomena most surprising to the foreigner in Athens: this centuries-old city is a mushroom town, a new town embracing a few, scattered, precious memories of the past. The Acropolis is drowned in the immense agglomeration. The Corinthian columns of the Olympeion seem quite slender at the end of the vast Syngros boulevard. Rome or Istanbul, Florence or Paris have lived a continuous existence, where each phase has left its traces. In the history of Athens there is a sort of hiatus of several centuries, a parenthesis of nothingness. There is no transition from Byzantine churches to concrete flats, apart from a few official buildings and some increasingly rare houses of outmoded charm, dating from the reign of King Otho.

The growth of Athens was accelerated after 1923 when a million and a half refugees from Asia Minor, deprived of all their possessions and needing shelter, food and employment, were repatriated into a Greece incapable of supporting its own population. Many settled around Athens. The city was enlarged with hurriedly constructed suburbs which were baptized with nostalgic names such as New Ionia and New Smyrna. In addition, in 1944 the civil war attracted an influx of provincials towards the capital in search of security or employment. Thus a populous agglomeration grew up, extending to the dimensions of a capital. It is very far now from the captive, rustic Athens which excited Lamartine and Byron, or from the bourgeois administrative centre which Edmond About maliciously parodied. Transformed within a few years, pierced by vast avenues, enlarged by new districts which scale the slopes of Hymettus and the Pentelicon, Athens has become one of the most beautiful cities of the Mediterranean.

Arrival at Athens by plane at night is an exciting sight: a scintillating cloth, stretching as far as the eye can see, the city covers as much space as towns with three or four times as many inhabitants. In daytime, one sees at a glance the rectangular plain which encloses Athens with its suburbs and the port of Piraeus. To the south is the sand-fringed sea. Face to face rise Mount Hymettus, bare beneath odorous bushes, and Mount Parnes crowned with fir trees. The triangle of the Pentelicon blocks the horizon to the north: patches of snow on the blue slopes mark the source of the marble from which the Parthenon was constructed. Between the Pentelicon and Hymettus a pass leads towards the plain of Marathon. To the south of Parnes, a pass leads towards the plain of Eleusis. Athens is conveniently sheltered by mountains, and yet retains access to the sea and its neighbours.

Towards the Pentelicon, Athens is both rustic and fashionable. The elegant villas of Kifissia and Psychico shelter beneath green shrubbery. Vines, olive trees and corn are grown in the fields of red clay, which the potters, as in olden times, make into vases. Nearer the sea the town becomes more densely populated and the soil tawny like the pelt of a lion: Athens seems to be lying on a desert. On the periphery, the small white, blue or pink square buildings of the refugee quarter are still dispersed along roads as yellow and battered as the bed of a rushing stream. The centre is a compact chaos cut by long shining avenues, with the park of Queen Amelia standing out as a green, and the Pan-Athenian Stadium as a white patch. The Lycabettos is a sharp peak, with its base hidden by the geometrical layout of large blocks of new flats: the aristocratic quarter of Kolonaki. The Acropolis and the old quarter of Plaka are seen as a rocky tableau surrounded by a village, and with a magnificent temple balanced on top. Then, stretching like a cord from the Acropolis to the coast is Syngros Avenue, aflower with oleanders. There is the lawn of the Hippodrome. To the right, towards Mount Parnes and Salamis, are the taverns of Phaliron where in the summer plaintive *bouzoukias* are sung, and then there are the hills of Piraeus. To the left, towards Mount Hymettus are the crowded beaches of New Phaliron, Ellenikon airport, the villas, the elegant beaches of Vouliagmeni and Glyfada, the splendid boulevard along the sea front, continued by the coastal road leading to Cape Sunion which will soon, by way of the north coast, make a complete circuit of Attica.

Athens is centred around two squares—Syntagma (Constitution) and Omonia (Concord)—joined by three large parallel avenues. These were recently baptized Venizelos, Roosevelt and Churchill but the Athenians continue to use their old names—Academy, University and Stadium. Syntagma, situated near the residential quarters of Kolonaki and also the Avenue of Queen Sophia with its fringe of ministries and embassies, not far from the royal palace and Herodes Atticus Street shaded by pepper plants, is aristocratic and cosmopolitan. The vast quadrilateral, bordered by travel agencies and large hotels, hums with intense activity. When night falls and the square is lit by neon advertisements the promenade is covered by tables and canvas chairs. In the evening freshness, the Athenians meet to eat ices or drink coffee or the beautifully coloured cherry syrup, *vyssinade*. Syntagma is dominated by the old royal palace, now used as the Chamber of Deputies. Built without grace but also without pretension, it forms a fitting backcloth to the tomb of the Unknown Soldier. This is guarded by two sentries who emerge mechanically and at fixed intervals from their sentry boxes to execute an irreproachable and complicated manœuvre with the precision of a Swiss cuckoo clock. On Sundays, the changing of the guard takes place to music and is particularly picturesque when the royal guard, the *evzones*, in red caps, white fustanellas and *tsaroukias* with large pompoms on their feet, take over.

In contrast to Syntagma, Omonia is fundamentally Athenian. The change in character takes place half-way between the two squares; the limit of the zones is marked by the university buildings in neo-classical style. The shops along the three roads suddenly become less luxurious and more utilitarian. The European *pâtisserie* is replaced by the *Zacharoplaste*, the 'modeller in sugar', offering syrupy cakes decorated with cinnamon and honey in great zinc moulds —the bearded *kataif* or the flaky *baklava* with its nutty flavour. The restaurant becomes the tavern where lambs' intestines turn in the shop-window—*cocoretsia* in long twists on a horizontal spit; and exquisite *kebab* on a vertical spit for consumption with beer, raisin wine or *ouzo*. The immense Patissia Avenue, which ran through open country a hundred years ago, today crosses a rich quarter inhabited by ship-owners, and houses the National Museum and the Polytechnic School. But Omonia belongs essentially to the popular and thickly populated districts. The mouths of the Underground railway to Piraeus open in the heart of the square. The business streets of Eolou and Athena, where the crowds are so dense that a vehicle can scarcely make its way through them, run down to the Acropolis and enclose the *agora*, the covered market. Here, on the eve of Easter the sight of thousands of lambs hanging amidst baskets of red eggs is unforgettable. In Holy Week, an uninterrupted line of stalls springs up in the centre of the road offering decorated candles, icons, and copper perfume-pans emitting heavy fumes of incense to passers-by. Rows of painters, their brushes fixed to long sticks, wait near pails of whitewash for clients who want houses or pavements whitened to celebrate the Resurrection in a fitting manner.

Eolou ends in the Monastiraki quarter. Here is the Athens of engravings, an Athens seen by the travellers in the eighteenth century, an Athens which mixes antiquities and Turkish innovations with its everyday life. Workmen in copper are grouped in Hephaistos Street, moulding the feet of candelabras for churches, hammering baptismal bowls or the large circular platters used by innkeepers. Not far away, rubber merchants pile up old tyres against the Corinthian columns of the Library of Hadrian from which the shoemakers of Pandrosa Street—or Babouches Street—cut their soles. Narrow, smelling of leather and dye, Babouches Street offers the passer-by a multitude of shoes hanging in bunches from the fronts of booths. Here and there one sees the bric-à-brac of an antique-dealer's shop-window. The ancient mosque transformed into an art gallery and an old Turkish bath add their touch of oriental colour. Nearer to the Acropolis are small quiet squares, dozing in the gentle shade of the pepper plants, disused houses, with façades decorated with fake Corinthian pilasters, russet-tiled roofs edged with terra-cotta palm leaves—the Athens of sixty years ago. Here is the hydraulic clock in white marble, the Tower of the Winds, decorated with winged figures and constructed in the first century AD by the Macedonian engineer, Andronicos. Here also, in romantic abandon amidst bushes, is the bluish marble of the Roman *agora*. These monuments of the 'early period' are now judged more fairly than hitherto. Their proximity does not detract from the nearby Acropolis. Its imposing vertical frontage rises behind them, crowned by the wall that Themistocles had hastily erected with the debris of buildings ravaged by the Persians. Cylindrical marble drums and great blocks of frieze are recognizable amongst the fittings, displayed by the victors for all to see as eternal witness to Medean barbarism.

Imperceptibly, Monastiraki gives way to Plaka, the provincial to a village preserved in the heart of a great city: steep roads, Montmartre-like stairways, popular taverns filling the roadway with their odour of frying and their iron tables. And a few minutes from enormous blocks of flats stand fragile country houses, whitewashed *spitakia* with blue shutters on their white walls, a tethered goat cropping the sparse grass on wasteland hung with washing. And always there is the grey and red cliff of the Acropolis hollowed out by caves, bristling with cactus.

There are few places in Athens whence the Acropolis is not visible. Nature has placed it in the Athenian countryside in the same way as a pedestal is isolated in the middle of a museum to enhance a particular treasure and offer it for all to admire. To the sailor, the Acropolis seems very small, as if absorbed in the surrounding city. From Lycabettos it rises sharply above the disorder of houses to dominate the sea where the triangle of Aegina points to the horizon. At sunset the magnificent sight of the illuminated marble Parthenon can be seen from the hill of Daphni against the violet slopes of Hymettus. To possess this steep rock is to hold at mercy Athens and Attica. Although it is also a sanctuary and a museum, the Acropolis is above all a strategic position: this fact did not escape the English parachutists who landed in Attica in 1944 during the civil war. They left some marks slightly whiter than the old scars on the columns of the Parthenon. Eighteenth-century travellers knew an Acropolis transformed into a fortress; watched over by janissaries, they sketched the marble jostled by casemates and slums. The stones of the Temple of the Wingless Victory were scattered in the parapet of a battery; a high Venetian tower accentuated the general military impression. This tower was destroyed by archaeologists: Barrès, who thought that it was Frankist, complained of it to a member of the French School of Athens who had been given the task of showing him round. Barrès was not a particularly gracious subject. Immersed in his obsessions, he climbed the Acropolis in search of the palace of the French dukes of Athens and, disappointed at his lack of success, gave free vent to his indignation. His guide took a malicious pleasure in encouraging this and persuaded the great man that it was intended to demolish the Parthenon in order to see what was underneath. This story is told in Barrès' *Voyage de Sparte*.

The first great excavation of the Acropolis was undertaken in 1852 by a member of the French School of Athens named Beulé. He used up 'fifty pounds of powder' to remove the Turkish bastions and discovered the top of the Byzantine postern that today bears his name several yards below the ground. He thought that he had unearthed the real entrance to the Propylaea. As he was not averse to a little honest advertising he had the particulars of his exploit engraved on an antique marble stele. Never has an archaeological blunder acquired such fame.

Today the visitor no longer enters the Acropolis by the Beulé Door but by a path which follows the exact outline of the old Sacred Way and skirting the bastion of the temple of Athena Nike, ends at the Propylaea. The Propylaea of Mnesicles formed a monumental porch. Its severe beauty, derived from architecture alone, won the unanimous admiration of the ancient peoples. They praised the dexterity with which the architect overcame the difficulties of the site, the masterly equilibrium of the marble architraves forced to span large expanses without breaking beneath their burdens, and, above all, its finesse— which would not escape a people subtle above all else—the play of the black and white steps designed to maintain the unity of proportions between a base of a constant height and the columns of varying heights in the façade and wings. The Propylaea of Mnesicles replaced the narrow entrance constructed at the time of the tyrants. Like two welcoming arms, they are symbolic of the generous and triumphant democracy of the fifth century opening at the entrance to the civic sanctuary, which Pericles dreamt of making into a sanctuary common to all Greeks.

When the Athenians returned to their ruined Acropolis after the victory of Plataea they were faced with a problem: should they be faithful to the promise made before the battle never to reconstruct the temples destroyed by the barbarians, in order to perpetuate the memory of their godlessness? However, the burnt stump of the sacred olive tree gave birth to a green shoot two cubits high; the omen vouchsafed by the goddess put the city on the road to renewed creation. The debris was swept up. The young girls sculptured in marble, consecrated to the goddess and mutilated by the invaders, were buried in a vast ditch as if in reserve for the museums of the future. So too were the smiling *cores* elaborately attired, the monsters of *poros*, lions and bulls, the good-humoured or brutal characters touched up in bright colours, which decorated the pediments of the archaic temples. Athens buried the past and went resolutely forward. Nothing was remade; everything was created. The Acropolis was the happiest solution ever conceived to the problems of post-war reconstruction.

One should re-read in translation the *Life of Pericles*, the part where Plutarch describes the feverish enthusiasm which inspired the work. Supreme control logically was in the hands of a sculptor, Phidias: indeed the great statue of Athena in gold and ivory had to govern the arrangement of the Parthenon constructed to shelter it. This did not come about without difficulties: they were surmounted, we know how happily, by the architects Ictinos and Callicrates. Up to September 26, 1687, the Parthenon was almost intact, as complete as the Theseion is today. The Count of Koenigsmark, who served in the Venetian army at the time of the siege of Athens, tells in his memoirs of the dramatic council of war which decided that a cannon should be aimed at the temple, transformed into a gunpowder factory by the Turks. At seven o'clock in the evening a cannon-ball produced the explosion. The Turkish garrison surrendered. Then followed the dismembering. Morosini, who led the Venetian troops, in a clumsy attempt at pillage, massacred the pediments which had been spared destruction. The scaffolding broke and the colossal marbles shattered on the rock. The Count of Choiseul-Gouffier carried a piece of the frieze and two metopes salvaged from the debris back to the Louvre; Lord Elgin dismantled the remaining pediments and the sculptured frieze. Unobtrusive restorations have saved whatever remained of the stripped temple.

Outlined against the sky, its marble golden on a blue base, the Parthenon today possesses a new beauty, very different from what its architects intended. Conceived as a solid form, it is nothing more than an airy silhouette. Between the Parthenon and its ruin, there is the same difference as between a living fern and its elegant but disembodied imprint left fossilized on a rock. However, such as it is, with the supple curve of its pedestal, with its columns slightly distended as if by muscles, bronzed by innumerable suns, this 'temple to Minerva' evokes no thought of death. The prophets and angels fading on its walls, the pedestal of the minaret which surmounted it at the time of the catastrophe stand witness to the fact that men conscious of its grandeur, despite the injuries of which the scarred columns give evidence, could never imagine that the masterpiece of Ictinos would cease to be a divine dwelling. The Acropolis to them will always be divine, as at the time when Pallas-Athene stood armed in her temple while the daylight outside, penetrating through the open door and diffused by a thin layer of water on the ground before the statue, made the ivory and gold goddess glisten in the semi-darkness beneath the ceilings of precious woods.

The Erechtheum has suffered much from its mishaps—certainly less from being a harem than as a Byzantine church, the organization of which brought disorder to a climax in a complicated design. The architect had to take into account the great difference in the level of the ground between east and west and include in a single building dispersed places of worship. Did the building not hold an old Athena carved in olive wood believed to have fallen from heaven, to which the city used to offer the *peplos* woven by the young Athenian girls every four years at the time of the Great Panathenaea? And when Athena and Poseidon quarrelled over sovereignty in Attica, it was on the site of the temple that the god hit the rock with his trident and the goddess made the olive tree of peace rise up. Phidias represented all this—the procession of the Panathenaea and the divine dispute—on the pediments and the frieze of the Parthenon, as if to bind the new temple of the victorious democracy to the most ancient past of Athens. But the Erechtheum sheltered the relics and the Athenians retained the custom of calling it 'the old temple' although it was reconstructed after the Parthenon. The legendary kings, Erechtheion, Cecrops, were worshipped there, as well as Pandrose, the daughter of Cecrops, who offered herself as a victim to the goddess and threw herself from the ramparts to save the besieged town. The precious shrine of the Erechtheum sets up her Ionic grace against the Doric vigour of the Parthenon, and her caryatids, as robust as columns and as supple as young girls, perpetuate the memory of the archaic *cores*. But these *cores* no longer simper: dignified and grave in their Dorian *peplos*, they disdain to seek admiration; they impose it.

The temple of Athena Nike or of the Wingless Victory, perched on its solid bastion, the result of a double restoration, today greets the visitor at the entrance of the Acropolis. As long ago as 449, the Athenians were asking Callicrates, one of the architects of the Parthenon, for an estimate which can still be read, engraved on marble at the Epigraphic Museum. However, work on the project only began in 427. Between 424 and 1686, the temple was an object of admiration of every traveller. Then the Turkish garrison dismantled it to build defence works. Lord Elgin extracted four blocks of sculptured frieze, an Ionic capital and a capital of a pilaster from the masonry and these were sent to the British Museum. In 1836, three German scholars discovered the blocks in the Turkish rampart and patiently reconstructed Callicrates' work. The architect and archaeologist, A. K. Orlandos, had to dismantle it and remount it again in 1936 following subsidence of the bastion. It was noticed on that occasion that the temple occupied the site of a still older sanctuary, apparently constructed to commemorate the battle of Plataea. These venerable remains are now accessible under the concrete platform which supports the temple.

Compact but elegant, refined yet vigorous, it is decorated with a sculptured frieze which probably represents the battle of Plataea. This decoration, the most ancient example of a historic frieze bequeathed by Greek art, joined the new temple to the sanctuary that it replaced. Golden Victories crowned the corners of the frontons. Victories preparing to offer a sacrifice were sculptured in bas-relief on the parapet which surrounded the bastion. They include the Victory removing her sandal, a marvel of equilibrium and grace, which is known the world over.

Previously, the now denuded Acropolis was crowded with ex-votos, more numerous than could be imagined, were it not for the marks cut in the bluish rock. Everybody in the city demonstrated his piety by some gift—a pensive Athena languishing on a small marble stele or the colossal bronze of the goddess consecrated by the settlers in Lemnos. An abbreviated catalogue of this immense collection remains in the work of Pausanias and some splendid remnants can be seen in the Museum of the Acropolis.

Lodged in the very heart of the sacred rock, the museum has the double advantage of not in any way spoiling the site and of preserving the master-pieces of archaic art and of the fifth century which are its glory at the places where they were discovered. If it has none of the profuse wealth of the National Museum, it contains nothing but the finest flower of Greek art. We advise the visitor to look first at the works of the fifth century on his right, friezes and metopes from the Parthenon, small white statues on a dark-blue base from the frieze of the Erechtheum, the wonderful parapet of the Victories. In fact, it is more profitable to go backwards in time and finish in the rooms of archaic sculpture. Those coloured frontons where lions bury their brutal fangs in the flesh of bulls crushed beneath their weight, where serpent-like monsters unroll the scaly coils of their muscular bodies, and those smiling or grave statues of young girls, the innocent Moschophore or the Zeus enthroned with the gravity of an oriental king, create an impression of simple, architectural power which would make the chisel of Phidias himself seem almost affected.

And even after visiting the major monuments spared by history there is yet another beautiful sight to contemplate, not on the Acropolis, but its surroundings: all Athens can be seen spreading out to the sea, blocked by Aegina and the mountains of the Peloponnese, but open towards the Cyclades. It is difficult to say at what time the view makes the greatest impression: in the fresh joyfulness of morning or the luminous majesty of evening, when the sun setting on Corinth opposite the violet Hymettus justifies the name given to the sunset by the Greeks: *Heliou Basileuma*, the Royalty of the Sun.

All that remains of ancient Athens is visible from the Acropolis. To the west a green space near an unfinished church marks the site of the Ceramic Cemetery. In accordance with the old custom the line of tombs stretches along the road which leaves the town by the double-gate, the Dipylon, and leads towards Eleusis. Today, as of old, this road joins Athens to the rest of Greece. It was therefore much frequented and the cemetery much in demand by people seeking ostentation even in death. It was there that Athens erected the tombs of her great men and the soldiers who died for her, that their memory might serve as an example to all. The two triumphs of Attic funeral art, the great vases of the eighth century BC and the sculptured steles of the classical epoch prevail in the necropolis. The 'geometric' vases of the Dipylon are not only a triumph for the technical dexterity of the potter, able to make such monumental items, or for the ingenuity of the decorator who could make such a range of varieties from his limited ornamental repertoire. The funeral scenes represented on these curving vases are also historical documents of the first order. To see all the armed warriors of a family in their chariots following behind the funeral chariot of these Eupatrides is to understand why Solon reduced by law the funeral extravagances two centuries later. When somebody died, these aristocrats organized veritable mobilizations and formed a perpetual menace to the State.

The marble steles of the classical epoch deserve to stand as a symbol of Atticism itself. The characters with pure profiles, one might call them hand-chiselled silhouettes, express the grief of separation with a restraint which makes them all the more moving. The Attic artist, like the god of Delphi, 'neither displays nor conceals: he signifies'. Funeral art has never been further removed from vulgarity.

The great procession of the Panathenaea formed up near the Dipylon and reached the Acropolis by crossing the *agora*, the civic and religious centre of the city. Previously chaotic and abandoned, the *agora* today has become a garden where ancient ruins of monuments razed to the ground, but dug up in the minute excavations of the American School, are shown against a background of trees and flowers. The *agora* is reduced to one level. Fortunately, two buildings offer some vertical relief amidst these two-dimensional antiques: the Stoa of Attalos and the 'Temple of Theseus'. Almost intact, the Temple of Theseus (actually not of Theseus but of Hephaistos, god of the iron workers) is the most unfairly disparaged of Greek buildings. Tourists, who have exhausted their capacity for enthusiasm on the Acropolis, call this little brother of the Parthenon, this twin of the temple of Cape Sunion, academic and artificial. They are indifferent to the warm colour of its golden marble and the beauty of its harmony with which the fifth-century Athenian endowed all his creations.

Opposite the temple of Hephaistos are the two storeys of white columns in Pentelicon marble of the Stoa of Attalos. American archaeologists have reconstructed it to serve as a museum for excavations from the *agora* as well as to form a screen to separate the present town and the antique quarter. The King of Pergamum, Attalos II, offered this monumental present to the city where he studied philosophy as a young prince. Shops now transformed into museum rooms, where the discoveries of the American archaeologists are clearly and tastefully displayed, opened beneath the colonnades and from the steps strollers could see the panorama of the *agora*. This large-scale architecture in proximity to the more ancient monuments must have made the same impression as the modern flats fifty years ago next to the bourgeois houses. Although of the 'late period', it is not devoid of merit. Compared with a capital of the Parthenon, a capital of the Stoa of Attalos seems arid and slovenly. But it is hardly fair to judge monuments conceived in such different spirits by the same criteria. The architects of the Hellenistic and Roman epochs saw their work as a whole. They were concerned with the functional study of plans, with the organization of large-scale ornamental rhythms; they disdained the details of orders and styles. On the other hand in a fifth-century temple each stone was cut with love, and carved like a work of art in its own right. Thence comes the pleasure in touching a piece of marble where one can feel the precision of the chisel. Destroyed, the Hellenistic building is only a ruin, the classical building becomes an anthology.

In a line to the south of the Acropolis are the restored Odeon of Herodes Atticus, the sanctuary of Aesculapius, the enormous colonnade of the King of Pergamum, Eumenes, and finally, paved with marble of the Roman epoch, the theatre of Dionysos with its snub-nosed Sileni. The plays given there at the Dionysiac Festival took the form of a competition between the dramatic poets. The richest citizens, appointed as leaders of the chorus, had to meet the expenses of the performance. The *choragus* whose chorus was honoured as winner received a tripod which he consecrated to Dionysos on a pedestal of varying degrees of sumptuousness. Of these 'chorus' monuments—so numerous at the time of Pausanias that the road which led to the theatre was called the Road of the Tripods—there only remains the exquisite rotunda consecrated by Lysicrates. Known in the Middle Ages as the 'lantern of Demosthenes', it was walled up for a long time in a monastery of French Capuchin friars, who ensured its safety. Transformed into a cell, it was shown on old engravings, occupied by a studious monk. One of the friars bought it from a Greek who was not the actual owner. A lawsuit was brought before the Turkish Cadi and won by the Capuchin on condition that he maintained the monument in good condition and allowed tourists to visit it. Lord Byron, it is said, slept there one night.

With its bunches of leafy Corinthian columns, the great temple of Olympian Jupiter was started by the tyrant Pisistratus six centuries before Jesus Christ at the beginning of the rise of Athens and finished eight centuries later by the Emperor Hadrian. Although Pisistratus was a tyrant, he died a natural death and his passing was even regretted. The Athenians were grateful to him for making Athens into an intellectual capital able to compete with the other great cities of the time, Corinth or Miletus. They even forgave his underhand dealing: driven from Athens by political forces, he returned to his petrified fellow citizens one day in the company of Athena herself driving him in her own chariot. One gathers from the sequel that the goddess was in reality a buxom flower girl helmeted for the occasion. Nothing was held against him. In the land of Ulysses cunning enchants even its victims.

The Olympeion is the last of the great pagan monuments of Athens. Christianity moved into the temples of the old gods and covered the town with new churches, of which some have survived. They have in common their small stature. But since the Temple of the Wingless Victory, Atticism has never forgotten that the monumental is attained less by magnitude of proportion than by harmonious balance. This is effectively illustrated by the proximity of the enormous church of the modern Metropolis and the little Metropolis. The little Metropolis is more attractive than the church of St Theodore or the Kapnikaraea buried under the earth of Hermes Street. The elegant dome, decorated frontons, the old marble reliefs embedded in the walls with their warm patina—they all create the impression of a museum piece produced by the delicate fantasy of a workman in ivory.

The past of Athens and of Greece also lives again in the numerous museums of the city. Three of them, the National Museum, devoted to antiquity, the Byzantine Museum and the Benakis Museum, which is essentially concerned with modern history, folk-lore and the popular arts, give a complete panorama of Greek civilization from pre-history to modern times. Entirely reorganized since the war under the impetus of its directors, Mr and Mrs Karouzos, the National Museum presents a dazzling collection of old sculpture, ceramics and jewellery, gathered at Athens itself and at various large sites which did not have their own museums at the time the objects were discovered. Thus, from the entrance, against the red background of the windows, the gold of Mycenae sparkles, masks and jewels exhumed by Schliemann. In the sculpture room, the Amazon of Epidaurus gambols and the 'Epioné' by the sculptor Timotheos, which previously decorated the crest of the temple of Aesculapius, descends from the sky, as graceful as a figure by Botticelli. There could be no question of giving even a summary description of these riches here. From the idols of the Cyclades to the statues of the Roman period, they comprise pieces of exceptional value and universal fame, such as the stele from Hegeso or the large bronze Zeus with its reddish-brown patina, which a fisherman caught in his nets one day in the open Euboea.

Leaving the museums, the visitor should also wander on the hills of Athens: on the Areopagus where the oldest council sat, the criminal court where gods and legendary heroes guilty of murder were judged. Orestes appeared before this tribunal and the tragedy of Aeschylus which has Orestes as its hero takes place on the Areopagus. An isolated block can still be seen which might have been the 'stone of offence' where the accused stood, or the 'stone of resentment' for the prosecutor.

Demosthenes and the illustrious Attic orators once spoke on the hill of Pnyx where the assembly of the people was held. The little Pnyx was the name sometimes given to the Hill of the Nymphs, also a place of reunion. Finally, the Hill of the Muses, the Mouseion, is crowned by the monument of Philo-pappos erected by the Athenians in the second century AD in honour of a Syrian prince, a benefactor of Athens.

The visitor should also wander in the Athenian suburbs, on the slopes of Hymettus, around the village chapel of St John the Hunter or the oasis of Kaisariani, if only to contemplate from on high this great animated city. The name Athens previously applied to the whole state (*polis*) astride the Attic penin-sula not, as today, only to the urban agglomeration (*astu*). Bounded on two sides by the sea, cut off from Boeotia on the third by the mountain chain of Citheron, three-quarters of this large area is occupied by arid mountains, the homeland of goats, coal-mining and the marble industry. The fertile plains of Marathon, Eleusis and Mesogaea could not have fed the population of ancient Athens. Its destiny was determined by its geography. Either it became imperialist or it did not exist at all. It became vigorously imperialist. But it should not be forgotten, when judging it for this, that the tribute it forcibly extorted from its 'allies' served to finance the monuments of the Acropolis and the marble temples scattered throughout Attica at that time.

A magnificent figure-head at the tip of Attica, the temple of Poseidon on Cape Sunion, now seems quite near Athens, as a result of the beautiful coastal road recently opened. Whipped by the salt wind, standing on its pedestal of rock, this fifth-century temple now flooded with visitors succeeds in preserving the grandeur and poetry it possessed when it was discovered in its solitude. The site of Rhamnonte is still—but for how long?—protected by its isolation. The ruins of the two temples of Nemesis, the goddess who punished inordinate pride, are still visible beside the fortress standing on the north-east coast opposite Euboea to protect the passage of the convoys of grain. Xerxes, the King of the Persians was one of Nemesis' victims. The second temple, possibly constructed by the same architect as the temple of Sunion, was an offering by the Athenians to the divinity who saved them from his incursions. Artemis also was honoured on the north-east coast in the sanctuary of Brauron which has been recently excavated. The Persians probably destroyed the old temple. A new sanctuary was reconstructed in the fifth century with a temple, a monu-mental altar and a curious bent portico where the young Athenian girls who served the goddess, 'the bears' took their meals together. Thus, from one end of Attica to the other blossomed the sanctuaries to the gods.

50. Arrivée à Athènes.
a Porte d'Hadrien et
jardin de la Reine Amélie.
u fond, le Lycabette.

50. Arrival at Athens.
Hadrian's Arch and the
Garden of Queen Amelia.
In the background, Lycabettos.

50. Ankunft in Athen.
Das Hadrianstor und der Garten
der Königin Amelia.
Im Hintergrund: Der Lycabettos.

51. Athènes.
Place du Syntagma
et l'Acropole.

52-53. Evzones
montant la garde
devant le Palais
Royal.

51. Athens.
Syntagma Square
and the Acropolis.

52-53. Evzones mounting
guard in front of
the royal palace.

52
53

51. Athen.
Syntagma-Platz
und die Akropolis.

52-53.
Soldaten der Leibgarde
(Eftzonen) vor dem
Königspalast.

54
55

56

57

54. *Rue de l'Athènes moderne.*
55. *Quartier de Monastiraki,*
rue des Babouches.
56. *Vendeur de « coulouria ».*
57. *Marchand d'éponges.*

54. *A street in modern Athens.*
55. *The Monastiraki quarter,*
street of the "babouches"
(oriental slippers).
56. *"Coulouria" seller.*
57. *Sponge merchant.*

54. *Straße im modernen Athen.*
55. *Monastiraki-Viertel,*
Straße der « Pantoffeln ».
56. *« Coulouria »-Verkäufer.*
57. *Schwammhändler.*

58

58. Odéon d'Hérode Atticus.
Sur la colline, monument
de Philopappos.
59. L'Acropole vue du
Mouseion (colline des Muses).

58. Odeon of Herodes Atticus.
On the hill,
the monument of Philopappos.
59. The Acropolis seen from the
Mouseion (Hill of the Muses).

58. Odeum des Herodes Attik.
Auf dem Hügel: Denkmal
des Philopappos.
59. Die Akropolis, vom Muse.
(Musenhügel) aus gesehen.

à 67.

E PARTHÉNON.

-64-65-66-67 :
rises du
rthénon.
itish Museum
3-64-67)
Musée de
Acropole
5-66).

61

61. Fronton est. Un des chevaux
de Séléné et Dionysos.
62. Fronton ouest. Fragments de
statues (Cécrops et sa fille Aglaure?).

61. Östlicher Ziergiebel
des Parthenon.
Dionysos mit einem Pferd.

- 67.

IE PARTHENON.

-64-65-66-67 :
ezes of the
rthenon.
tish Museum
3-64-67) and the
ropolis
seum (65-66).

61. East fronton: one of the horses
of Selene and Dionysos.
62. West fronton: fragments of statues
(Cecrops and his daughter Aglauros?)

62. Westlicher Ziergiebel:
Fragmente von Statuen
(Kekrops und seine
Tochter Aglauros?)

62

- 67.

RTHENON.

-64-65-66-67 :
es des
thenon.
isches
seum
-64-67)
Museum
Akropolis (65-66).

63

64

67

63. *Offrande du péplos à Athéna.*
64. *Centaure enlevant une femme Lapit*
65. *Métèques portant des hydries.*
66. *Préparation du sacrifice à Athén*
67. *Les cavaliers athéniens à la process*

63. *Opfergaben für Athene.*
64. *Kentaur entführt eine Lapitheny*

65

. Offering of the peplos to Athena.
. Centaur carrying off a woman of the Lapithae.
. Metecs carrying hydriae.
. Preparation for the sacrifice to Athena.

. Athenian horsemen in procession.

66

-66. Vorbereitung zur Opferung für Athene.
. Athenische Reiter bei der Prozession.

69
70

L'Erechthéion.
Tribune de l'Erechthéion,
Caryatides.
Musée de l'Acropole.
ctoires ailées conduisant
génisse au sacrifice.

69. *The Erechtheum,*
Caryatids.
Acropolis Museum.
nged Victories leading
heifer to the sacrifice.

69. *Erechtheion.*
enhalle des Erechtheion.
Museum der Akropolis.
lügelte Niken.

71

71. Temple d'Athéna Niké.
Musée de l'Acropole.
72. Victoire délaçant sa sandale.

71. Temple of Athena Nike.
Acropolis Museum.
72. Victory unlacing her sandal.

71. Tempel der Athena N
Akropolis-Museum.
72. Nike löst ihre Sandale

72

73. Musée de l'Acropole. La salle des Corés.   *73. Acropolis-Museum. Hall of the*

73. *Saal der Koren, Akropolis-Museum.*

75. Tritopator (fronton du vieil Hécatompédo

75. Tritopator (fronton of the old Hecatompea

Acrop

Musée de l'Acropole.

76. Fronton du temple des Alcméon

à Delphes: chevaux du char d'Apo

74

76

74. Athéna pensive.   74. Trauernde Athene.

74. Pensive Athena.

76. Fronton of the Alcmaeonid Ten

at Delphi: horses of Apollo's charie

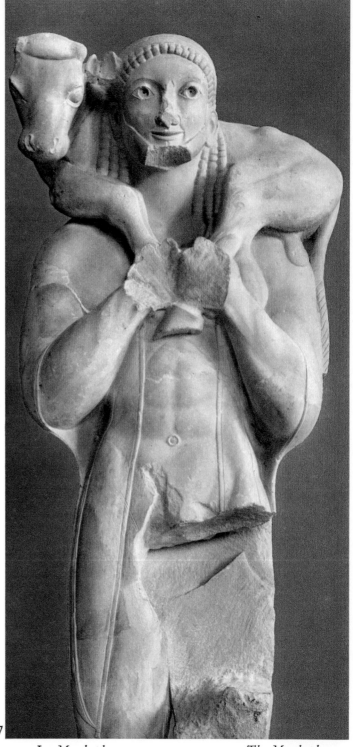

. Tritopator (Ziergiebel
alten Hekatompedon).

seum.

Akropolis-Museum.

. Ziergiebel des Alcmeonides-Tempels
Delphi: Pferde vom Wagen
Apollon.

77

77. Le Moschophore.   77. The Moschophoros.

77. Der sogenannte Kalbträger.

78. *Le stade panathénaïque.*
79. *Le portique d'Attale.*

78. *The Panathenaic Stadium.*
79. *The stoa of Attalos.*

78. *Panathenäisches Stadion.*
79. *Säulenhalle des Attalos.*

79

80

80-81. Nécropole du
Céramique.
Stèles funéraires.
82-83. Agora antique
et le temple d'Héphaïstos
(« Théseion »): 82. Eta
actuel et 83. reconstitutio

81

80-81. Ceramic Cemetery.
Funeral steles.
82-83. Ancient Agora and t
Temple of Hephaistos
(Theseion): as it is now,
and a reconstruction.

80-81. Nekropolis des
Kerameikon. Grabstelen.
82-83. Antike Agora und
Tempel des Hephaistos
(« Theseion »): jetziger Zust
und Rekonstruktion am Mod

82

83

84. *Le temple d'Héphaïstos* (« *Théseion* »).　　　　　*84. Temple of Hephaistos (Thesei*

85

85. Frise ionique de l'opisthodome (ouest).
86. Frise ionique du pronaos (est).

85. Ionic frieze from the opisthodomos (west).
86. Ionic frieze from the pronaos (east).

85. Ionischer Fries der Tempelrückseite (westlich).
86. Ionischer Fries der Vorderseite (östlich).

86

84. Tempel des Hephaistos (Theseion).

87. Le théâtre de Dionysos
vu de l'Acropole.

87. The Theatre of Dionysos
seen from the Acropolis.

87. Theater des Dyonysos
der Akropolis ausgesehen.

88

89

90

88-89-90. *Orchestra.*
Silènes ornant la scène.

88-89-90. *Orchestra:*
Ornemental Sileni.

88-89-90. *Bühnenvorraum.*
Silen-Statuetten als Sockel.

91
92

91. The monument of Lysicrates.
92. The Tower of the Winds.
93. The Little Metropolis.

91. Denkmal des Lysikrates.
92. Turm der Winde.
93. Kleine Metropolis.

94

Musée Byzantin.
94. L'Amour.
95. Saint Christophe le Cynocéphale.
96. Table à décor byzantin.

Byzantine Museum.
94. God of Love.
95. Saint Christopher the Cynocephalus.
96. Table with a byzantine decoration.

Byzantinisches Muse
94. Göttliche Liebe
95. Der hundsköpfi
St. Christoph.
96. Tisch mit bya
tinischem Ornament.

95

96

97. Musée national.
Salle des trésors de Mycènes.
98. Poignards mycéniens.

97. National Museum.
Hall of the Treasures
of Mycenae.
98. Mycenaean daggers.

97. Schätze aus dem
Grabhaus von Mykene
im Nationalmuseum
Athen.
98. Mykenische Dolche.

Musée National d'Athènes.   *National Museum of Athens.*   *Nationalmuseum Ather*
99. Cratère du Dipylon.   *99. Funeral urn from the Dipylon.*   *99. Krater aus Dipylo.*

Musée National d'Athènes.   National Museum of Athens.   Nationalmuseum Athen.

100. Stèle funéraire d'Hégéso.   100. Funeral stele of Hegeso.   100. Grabstele der Hegeso.

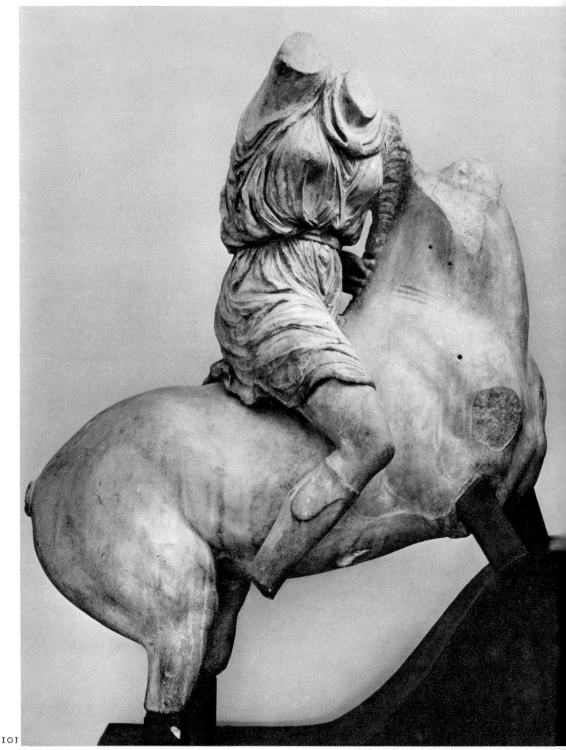

101. Penthésilée, reine des Amazones.
102. Niké ailée trouvée à Délos.
103. Apollon en bronze trouvé au Pirée.

101. Penthesilea, Queen of the Amaz[ons]
102. Winged Nike found at De[los]
103. Bronze Apollo found at the Pira[eus]

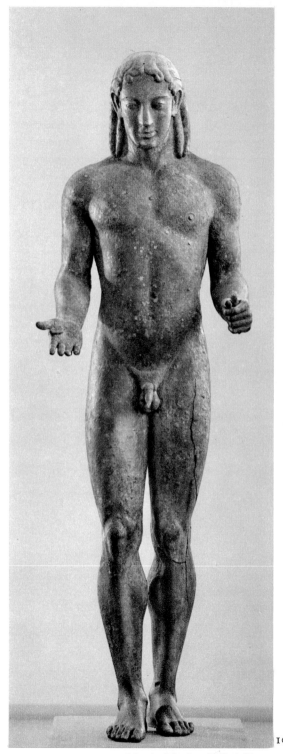

2

1. *Penthesilea, die Königin der Amazonen.*
2. *Geflügelte Nike, gefunden auf Delos.*
3. *Apollon aus Bronze, gefunden in Piräus.*

Musée National d'Athènes.
National Museum of Athens.
Nationalmuseum Athen.

104

105

106

107. *Musée National d' Athènes.*　　107. *National Museum of Athens.*　　107. *Nationalmuseum At*
Le Zeus de bronze de l' Artémision.　*The bronze Zeus from the Artemision.*　*Zeus aus Bronze, Artemis*

. *Temple de Poseidon*
cap Sounion.

108. Temple of Poseidon
at Cape Sunion.

108. Poseidontempel
auf Kap Sunion.

109

109. *Plage du Nouveau-Phalère.*   109. *Beach at New Phaliron.*   109. *Strandbad in Neu-Phali*

II. FROM ATHENS TO THE PELOPONNESE

UNTIL quite recently Athens was an almost exclusively maritime city. The ancient Athenians, masters of the seas, thought they had assured its security for all time by joining it to its harbour by long walls. Athens lived by virtue of Piraeus. Argolis and Macedonia sent it their products by sea from Salonika or Nauplia. The sudden development of road transport has changed this centuries-old situation. Athens is now joined to the rest of Greece by two new roads. A beautiful coastal road runs northwards round the straits of Euboea, passes Thermopylae, the valley of Tempe, skirts the foot of Olympus and ends at Salonika. Towards the Peloponnese, the old Corinth road has recently been joined by a motorway, and a heavy traffic of lorries brings fruit and early vegetables from Argos and Messenia every day. This broad thoroughfare reaches Daphni in a few minutes.

The fame of the antique monuments in Greece has always detracted from the Byzantine monuments. In their haste to arrive at Mycenae or Delphi, tourists only pay a short visit to Daphni. There, however, one can see the most beautiful examples of eleventh-century Byzantine art in Attica. In front of the church, a few yards from the noisy road, a paved courtyard stands bordered by cloisters with very low arches. An olive tree grows near a well. There is a large cypress, its trunk bare beneath dense foliage. Two thinner cypresses frame the side door leading into the nave. A marble Ionic column re-used in the porch remains as a reminder of the temple of Apollo Daphnephoros, 'Apollo of the Laurels', which preceded the church; while the outline of a Gothic arch, a sarcophagus marked with fleur-de-lys, are reminders of its occupation by the Cistercians in the thirteenth century, when the French dukes were in residence at the Acropolis. A monastic peace reigns here, conducive to idleness if not to meditation, instilling in the mind that basic minimum of laziness necessary to aesthetic contemplation.

Because of its size, Daphni possesses what Byzantine churches, compact beneath their domes, so often lack: interior space. It is not cluttered up with those silver chandeliers and lamps which destroy all sense of perspective and make the churches of Athens more pleasant from the outside than from within. The iconostasis panels which ordinarily separate the worshippers from the choir no longer exist. The walls are stripped of their marble covering except for a delicate cornice decorated with flowers and birds. This bareness sets off the elegant purity of the architecture.

The plan of Daphni follows the type known as 'the Engraved Greek Cross'. Greek religious architecture followed two types of plan. The first, an inheritance from Hellenistic architecture, is the basilica: a rectangular edifice divided lengthways into several naves by lines of parallel columns covered by a double-sloping roof. In fact, the basilica is a large hall perfectly adapted to its function of sheltering crowds. It is a practical and rational monument. The most famous example in Greece is the church of St Demetrius of Salonika.

But Byzantine architects were very impressed by the symbolic value of the dome, which originated in the East. Made in the image of the celestial vault, it seemed to them more worthy of covering a divine sanctuary than the common saddle-back roof, and more 'eloquent' to the worshippers, directing their gaze towards heaven. But the task of adapting a circular dome to the quadrilateral of a church presented great technical problems. These the architects solved by placing the dome at the intersection of two naves which cut each other at right angles, thus forming a cross. Between the branches of the cross, at the four corners are chapels which form a quadrilateral. These chapels, in their turn, are covered by roofs with frontons or by little domes. The roofs as much as the beautiful colours of the walls—red bricks or russet marble stones—contribute to the picturesque appearance of the Byzantine churches, giving them a toy-like charm.

The symbolism of the architecture is accentuated by that of the decoration, which was subject to a strict tradition. At a time when Greece was impoverished and less costly frescoes were in use, Daphni was decorated with mosaics of rare beauty. The All-Powerful, the Pantocrator Christ gleams at the top of the dome. Under the influence of the Italian Renaissance, western art has retained only the poetic or pathetic aspects of religion—Nativities, Madonnas, the Crucifixion. In the God who became a man, it sees predominantly the Man, while Byzantium strove to express the God. It never came so near success as in the Christ at Daphni, whose strength has never been equalled except perhaps in the art of a Rouault. The other characters in these mosaics, iridescent against a golden background, have an elegance which one might take for Florentine if it were not enough to call it Attic. The spirit of Athens animates the normally frigid silhouettes and gives the heavy robes the grace of ancient drapery. It smiles down upon the church plunged in meditation beneath the benediction of the fearsome Pantocrator.

From the heights of Daphni we descend to the Bay of Salamis, a water-colour in pale blue, its sweetness refreshing after the dusty aridity of the Athenian suburbs. Unfortunately industrial buildings abound at the back of the gulf. In a blurred distance, along the sea-shore, lies Eleusis, homeland of the poet Aeschylus, a small town without mystery, where pipes, paint and cement are manufactured: a completely new small town, amidst the oleanders, houses of reinforced concrete, stridently enamelled petrol stations, bundles of wires on wooden telegraph poles. The factories of Eleusis are not beautiful, though we must do justice to the great chimneys which rise like smoky torches round the sanctuary of Demeter.

Eleusis is undoubtedly the place in Greece where there is the most painful contrast between the beauty of a name, the grandeur of the memories which surround it like a halo, and the archaeological reality. A very ordinary grill encloses the ruins, previously hidden by high walls which the uninitiated could only pass through at risk of their lives. At the entrance, Anthony the Pious, hurled down from the propylaea where he used to decorate the fronton, now emerges from the waist upwards from a marble port-hole like a ticket-collector from his window. The large initiation room is reached through two propylaea, their flagstones worn down by millions of footsteps. It is reduced to marks on the earth, but the marble triglyphs lying on the grass give some idea of its size. Cut in the rock at the foot of the cliff are tiers of seats which held the crowds of initiated for many centuries, dazzled by sudden light from above, waiting for the appearance of the sacred objects, the beautiful corn-ear of Eleusis, rich with promise for the dreaded future after death. Those who had drunk the sacred beverage, and seen with their own eyes that which was hidden from common mortals, departed safe in their knowledge of the certain road to join the blissful throng after death. When they distrusted their memories, they engraved the details of the itinerary in a small poem on a golden lamina and took it with them to the grave. They had found their paradise in advance. The translation of the mystical formula reads: 'Kid, I have fallen into the milk!'

At the exit to Eleusis, the traveller finds two roads: straight ahead is the Citheron with bare wasteland, Boeotia, Delphi, northern Greece. To the left the road leads towards Megara and Corinth. The new motorway is cut straight across the sides of the mountain and tends to make one forget the ancient road. Yet those who are not in a hurry may still prefer the latter. It follows the intricacies of the coast along a sea front that seems almost a lake. At times it hugs the water, at others it dominates the sea from the heights of a precipice itself overhung by impressive cliffs. The brigand, Sciron, could not have chosen a more dramatic setting for the exercise of his trade. Towards Corinth, the passage widens, cut by torrents where bunches of oleanders shelter. On this dry ground, the wind allows only olive trees well anchored in the ground to grow, or pines which bend gently with the wind. The road approaches the canal of Corinth and the Peloponnese, passing wasteland and a hill of yellowy green excavated earth.

The Peloponnese lives true to its name of 'the Isle of Pelops' for the canal has cut the narrow isthmus which joined it to continental Greece. Pelops, on his way to Olympia, crossed the Gulf of Corinth in the west, without suspecting the existence of the Isthmus, and believed he had landed on an island which he called by his own name. This legend takes us back to the origins of Greek history, the continuous development of which from Atreus to

Kolokotronis can be followed in the Peloponnese. Each epoch is represented by monuments of incomparable value. Mycenae has her tombs and ramparts, the archaic period the old temple of Corinth, classicism the buildings of Phigalia, Epidaurus, Nemea and Tegaea; Olympia, like Delphi, begins and ends with Hellenism; Corinth is Roman, Mistra Byzantine and the rocky peaks of Elis, Argolis and Corinthia are topped with strong castles, dating back to the Middle Ages. The Greek countryside makes so strong an impression that it is always tempting to think that wherever you are is the most beautiful place. However, the countryside of the Peloponnese justifies the most lyrical descriptions. Bristling with mountainous masses whose names are made for poetry—Cyllene, Erymanthus, Menale, Taygetus, the Lyceum—its snow-capped summits, with sides of bare rocks or clothed with forests, often rise to over seven thousand feet. Savage Arcadia is surrounded by the orchards of Argos, Sparta and Messenia. The cliffs plunge into the sea along the roughly broken coastline, fringed with narrow beaches before a sea full of islands, or deserted as far as the eye can see.

Some twenty thousand feet broad and two hundred feet high, the Isthmus of Corinth, 'the bridge over the sea', as Pindar called it, between Greece and the Peloponnese, was also a very awkward barrier to navigation between Ionia and the rich cities of Magna Graecia and Sicily. Six centuries before the birth of Christ, Periander, tyrant of Corinth but also one of the Seven Sages, played with the project of cutting it by canal. But such an undertaking was not within reach of a Greek city. It was more on the Roman scale. Caligula's engineers studied a drawing which was so well calculated that the French company which continued their work in 1892 needed only to follow it. In 67, a golden shovel in his hand, Nero inaugurated the cutting. Six thousand men, legionaries and Jewish prisoners from Judea, pushed it well ahead. Five million cubic metres were cleared in four months. But Nero died and the work was interrupted. A small Heracles, sculptured on the rock of the south wall, marks the place where they stopped on the side of the Gulf of Corinth.

Lacking a canal, the ancient navigators had either to resign themselves to the perilous detour by the south of the Peloponnese, keeping clear of Capes Taenarus and Malaea, or to pass over the Isthmus with their boats and cargoes using a haulage system which the ancient texts call *diolcos*. A fortuitous discovery enabled the Society of Hellenic Archaeology in 1957 to exhume the important pieces of the imposing paved road which wound round the sides of the hill. Deep ruts hollowed in the stone mark the passage of platforms on wheels on which the vessels, temporarily leaving their sea route, journeyed between the two gulfs amongst the pines and sweet-smelling bushes.

At the opening of the Isthmus is the sanctuary of Poseidon, one of the four great pan-Hellenic sanctuaries. Its site was recently discovered and excavated by a mission from the University of Chicago. Unfortunately, the

Byzantines needed materials for a wall to bar the Isthmus against barbarian invaders and the sanctuary supplied them with a convenient quarry. As a result, all that remains of the beautiful temple is the design inscribed in the rock, reminiscent of the footprint of a vanished traveller in the sand.

Only two beauties remain in modern Corinth: its name, which has the sonorousness of bronze, and its gulf. Opposite the town, the mountain of Loutraki descends in a long cape where the lighthouse of Perachora is lit in the evening. Beyond, the horizon extends as far as the rocky masses of the Helicon and Parnassus which are so pale a blue in spring that they blend with the sky, leaving the snow-capped summits as though suspended in the azure. Corinthians scorn their magnificent sea front. For Sunday walks they prefer a wide avenue lined with houses built to withstand an earthquake, cafés and pastry-shops; lamb on the spit, made better there than anywhere else, so the Corinthians say, roasts on the pavement in iron braziers.

Before the earthquake of 1928, Corinth was built to the south-west of the present agglomeration, on the actual site of the ancient city at the foot of its acropolis, the Acrocorinth, with its indented battlements. Only a hamlet remains today, on the hill where ripens the vineyard which is said to supply the seedless raisins for the cakes of England. The sweet grapes are exposed to the sun on driers humming with wasps; in the evening long tents screen them from night-time humidity. From this village of old Corinth, the view over the gulf is still more beautiful. The site has the calm grandeur found so often in the Greek countryside. The intense luminosity is not blinding: the transparent mist blends the blues of the sky, the mountains and the sea with the yellow of the earth on which the bronzed green cypresses stand out clearly.

The destruction of Corinth by Mummius in the second century BC spared only a few Greek monuments. The oldest of the temples still standing, the temple of Apollo, raises its monolithic columns with their greatly widened capitals. The initiated will not forget to ask the caretaker of the museum for the keys to the little Greek fountain, intact under its Roman packing. To reach it is like descending into a catacomb. Water no longer flows from the muzzles of the verdigris-covered lions, but moss and fern palms grow in the gaps between the stones, maintaining a haven of delicious freshness under the sunburnt ruins. The most important ruins are grouped around the vast esplanade which the Romans under Augustus constructed round a large Greek portico, spared from the pillage of the city. The monumental tribune rises in the centre, flanked by marble exedras and small sanctuaries. It was before this tribune that in 51 the governor, Gallio, summoned the Apostle, Paul. His sermon, though a source of trouble in the town which held a numerous Jewish colony, none the less gave birth in Corinth to one of the oldest churches in Greece.

Practically nothing on the Acrocorinth recalls the sanctuary of Aphrodite-Astarte and its thousand courtesans. The castellated towers are more evocative of the Frankish conquest and the rough face of the Byzantine general who defended them for three years. This general, Leon Sgouros, fought with a club and had no scruples about hanging a bishop. Worn down by hunger, he donned his armour, mounted his horse and jumped into space before the citadel surrendered.

At Mycenae, one's welcome is very unlike what one would expect from a place which has seen so many dark dramas. A long alley, shaded by eucalyptus trees, leads from the main road to the modern village across fields of beautiful red earth, rich soil on which corn, barley and maize grow. After the harvest, goats and sheep graze on the stubble, while asses follow with their shaggy velvet-eyed foals in train.

Beyond the village, near the inn of Helen the Fair (Menelaus' Helen the Fair, specifies the sign-board!), the road rises, amidst oleanders, towards the acropolis of Mycenae. This seems minute at the foot of a stony gorge, mole-cast with pebbles, between the twin mountains rising at its sides like the two lionesses of its coat of arms. Beyond the Door of the Lionesses lies the circle of tombs where Schliemann in 1872 unearthed the Kings of Mycenae masked in gold from under ten yards of earth. A steep path leads through the debris, where anemones flower in the spring and which crackling grass turns russet in summer, to the palace of the Atrides. It is now a plan marked out on the earth. Then the path leads to the summit of the acropolis where the foundations of a Greek temple remain. The acropolis, that looks like an insignificant hillock from the distance, suddenly appears in its true form. A high watch-tower surveys the Argive plain, rich in cultivated fields and orange trees stretching to the sea. One can understand how such a situation attracted the Achaean kings, agriculturalists and sailors as they were, in search of an acropolis on which to build their palaces. These were surrounded by enormous walls, and were remarkable rather for the size of the blocks of stone than for their magnificence. Ulysses' wealth was the fast boat rowed by his companions, but also the hundreds of pigs fattened by the faithful Eumaeus in the Ithacan stables. The house of the oil merchant excavated at Mycenae in 1952 by English archaeologists, with his sealed jars still lined up in the cellars, clearly illustrates the rustic aspect of Achaean opulence. Near the jars, merchants' accounts were found engraved on thirty-nine clay tablets. At much the same time, almost a thousand similar tablets came to light at Pylos at the 'Palace of Nestor'. The writing, which no one could read, was of the type known as 'Linear B', already represented by tablets to be found only in Crete at Knossos. But it had always been generally thought that the Mycenaeans were ignorant of the practice of writing and that the rare tablets inscribed with 'Linear B' found in continental Greece were imported from more civilized Crete, and contained Cretan texts written in the Cretan alphabet. Cretan writing and language being equally unknown there was no hope of ever translating them. Suddenly, the large numbers of these tablets discovered at Mycenae and Pylos made the hypothesis of their Cretan origin very uncertain. Why should the Mycenaeans keep their accounts in a foreign language instead of in Greek? Two English scholars, Ventris and Chadwick, put forward the theory that the language on the tablets was Greek; applying the usual methods of decipherment to the Linear B writing, they succeeded in translating it. This was the greatest success in that field since the decoding of the Egyptian hieroglyphics by Champollion. Certainly, the contents of the tablets is not as interesting as a literary or historic text. Nevertheless, these modest accounts enable us to read Greek as it was spoken and written several hundred years before Homer. The presence of these tablets at Knossos suggests that, if the Achaeans did receive their first lessons from the Cretans, they also influenced them. In addition, the Hellenism of the Achaeans, generally considered as pre-Hellenes, can no longer be doubted. The Greeks today are understandably proud to see the history of their country extend its limits and gain seven centuries of pre-history.

The results of the excavations undertaken at Mycenae since 1951 by Greek archaeologists are equally brilliant: many sensational discoveries have enriched and sometimes upset our knowledge of Mycenaean civilization. In front of the Door of the Lionesses an unsuspected stone circle—analogous to the one surrounding the tombs excavated by Schliemann—sets the boundary of a necropolis, containing some fifteen tombs, each marked by a simple mound surmounted by an engraved stele. The graves hold the remains of the princes who reigned at Mycenae about 1600 BC and were buried with their golden bracelets, their arms of state with alabaster or ivory pommels, their richly decorated vases of precious metal or terra-cotta. An electrum mask and, better still, a cornelian with the head of a bearded man engraved on it show the features of the first Greeks whose image we possess. Not all these funeral furnishings are purely Mycenaean: a make-up box in the form of a swan cut in rock crystal was undoubtedly imported from the East.

From the fourteenth century BC tombs in the earth were replaced by monumental vaults in the shape of hives, cut into the sides of the mountain and preceded by a long corridor or *dromos* that was filled with earth after the funeral. The celebrated 'Treasury of Atreus' which could, by its date, be the tomb of Agamemnon, is a unique edifice of its kind. The enormous size of the mottled stone blocks is less astounding than the precision of their adjustment and the secret harmony of the dome. Stripped of interior ornamentation, this dome in its abstract nudity fulfils in advance the Platonic definition of beauty: 'by beauty of form, I do not understand the same as do the vulgar, for example the beauty of living bodies or their drawn reproduction. I am speaking of straight and curved lines, of surfaces and solids which derive from straight lines and from circles, with the help of compasses, rulers and set-squares. Because these forms are not like the others, beautiful under certain conditions, but always beautiful in themselves by their very nature, and they are a source of very particular pleasure.'

The Dorian invaders ruined Mycenae and made the prosperity of Argos. Some ten miles from Mycenae the two acropolises of Argos rise over the plain: Aspis rounded like an upturned shield, and Larissa, steep and surmounted by the castle of Guy de la Roche. Since 1952, the French School of Athens has resumed exploration of the site. There is no better evidence of the importance of Dorian Argos than the large painted vases of the geometric epoch found in the tombs of the necropolis, the contemporaries of the Athenian vases of the Dipylon, but distinguishable by their purely Argive style. The Athenian artist represented his scenes in a continuous band as on an Ionic frieze; the painters of Argos inscribed them in a framework similar to the metope of the Doric frieze; they were more carefully laid out. One of the most successful is a large vase with three feet, over a yard high, where two diagrammatic wrestlers face each other with a forcefulness suggestive of the most modern art.

An Argive warrior chief was buried in one of these tombs in the eighth century with his plumed helmet and bronze breast-plate. By his side lay six long iron spits—*obeloi* in Greek (whence comes the word obelisk or spit, ironically given to the monoliths of Egypt). These *obeloi* are none other than the first *obolus*, of which six made up a drachma, a term first applied to the 'handful' of ears of corn which the harvester grasped when he cut them with his sickle. These *obeloi* which were about three feet nine inches long were not easy to handle. As iron became more common, it fell in value and more and more *obeloi* were required to make even a modest purchase. Therefore the Greeks welcomed the use of minted money in the seventh century, invented by the Lydians and spread in Greece by the Aeginetans. In the classical period, only a few cities such as Byzantium still used 'iron money'.

The classical epoch has left few traces in Argos. The theatre is one of the largest in Greece, with its eighty-three tiers cut into the blue rock of Larissa, able to seat an audience of twenty thousand. An odeum and an imposing gymnasium of the Roman epoch have also just come to light. Admirable mosaics of the fifth century AD, deposited in the Museum of Argos, represent episodes in a falcon hunt and the twelve months of the year, each symbolized by a different personality: January is a consul celebrating his accession to office by distributing pieces of gold, February a hooded fox-hunter. A soldier points to the May-time swallow: it is the season for departure to the country. A September vintager holds a bunch of grapes and a carafe of fresh wine. The fantasy of these personifications shows the characteristic Byzantine style, similar to our own Romanesque art, whilst the mixed foliage of masks and medallions which frames the panels curiously heralds certain creations of the Italian Renaissance.

From Argos to Nauplia, the road crosses a vast orchard. Here, amidst orange and apricot trees, stand the gigantic walls of Tiryns and, blocking the horizon, the citadel of Nauplia. Unlike many Peloponnesian towns, which have no beauty other than their site, Nauplia contributes an urban charm of its own to its picturesque natural setting. The powerful cliff of the Palamedes' fort, bristling with cacti and fantastically crowned with high walls, and the low acropolis of Itch-Kale enclosed by Venetian ramparts, marked with the lion of St Mark, first capture the attention on entering the town after skirting the gulf amidst fertile fields and orchards of orange trees. In this martial setting, Nauplia leads the peaceful and dignified existence of a country town, twice a capital: of the French duchy of Argos for a century, in 1247; and from 1827 to 1834 of newly liberated Greece. What is attractive in Nauplia—and is rare in Greece, paradoxical though this may seem in such an old country—is that the town gives the impression of having a past. Most of the houses resemble those of the old quarters of Athens: there are the same iron balconies, the same façades with Ionic pilasters, the same roofs crested with terra-cotta palmettes. The *platia* is bordered by the arches of a robust Venetian building constructed in 1713 by Augustin Sagredo, turned into a museum. Less happily transformed, the small mosque opposite holds the audience of the Trianon cinema every evening, after having been, in its days of glory, the seat of the first Greek Parliament. Between the square and the ramparts, houses line the narrow streets, cut with stairways crying out for conspiracies and ambushes. It is easy to imagine the intrigues which, under the first governments of independent Greece, divided the military leaders, the middle classes of the islands, and the intellectuals and resulted in the assassination of John Capodistria by the Mavromichalis family near the church of St Spiridon in 1831. A wide promenade runs along the seashore, in front of the crenellated Bourtzi building, previously the house of the executioner, now a luxury hotel. On the other side of the gulf, the two acropolises of Argos rise up in front of the mountain chain which encloses the plain. Over the gulf, the sun sets with imperial magnificence and on summer evenings the quays lit by the neon lights of the cafés are invaded by Nauplians coming and going in their best clothes solely for the joy of being together in the salt-scented freshness.

In Argolis, as in many places in Greece, that phrase of André Gide's comes to mind: choosing consists less in selecting than in excluding. The pleasure experienced never entirely wipes out the regret for what is missed. One would like to visit the ruins of the sanctuary of Hera, the Argive goddess, the little churches of Plataniti or Merbaka, to lounge on the shores of the Bay of Asine and, after a bathe in the green water at the foot of the promontory, to savour *ouzo* and *mezedes*, shaded by reed screens in the sea-front taverns.

But time presses on. Leaving Asine and its temptations behind on the right, we reach Epidaurus, nineteen miles beyond Nauplia. Leaving the plain of Argos we come upon sudden aridity, stony fields, prickly shrubs on rocks.

Large aloes coated with verdigris raise their yellow branches along the edge of the road—which leads to the splendid scenery of the Bay of Nauplia, its outlines picked out in every shade of grey and blue. Ligourio, the last village before the sanctuary of Aesculapius, possesses three country chapels, one of which, at the summit of the agglomeration, is decorated with ancient frescoes. From the road we greet the other two lying in the shade of almond trees. The tiers of the theatre of Epidaurus, embedded in the mountain beneath pine trees, are already in sight.

Apart from the theatre, all the monuments of the sanctuary, unearthed by the Hellenic Archaeological Society, are at ground level. The soft rock of the foundations is slowly splitting under its burden. But around the field of ruins, the pines, which perpetuate the memory of the sacred wood, maintain an odorous shade pierced by rays of sunlight where bees hum in the mornings. Epidaurus is a calm and peaceful park, the true home of Aesculapius, who was the good god of the ancient peoples. Aesculapius is one of the gods of Olympus, who had left the ranks, a former mortal who had been struck down by a thunderbolt from Zeus for having pushed his medical conscience to the extent of raising a man from the dead. Raised in his turn by the intervention of his father Apollo, he was placed amongst the ranks of the immortals, the most human and by far the most honourable of all. Accompanied by his wife and children he devoted himself to relieving the ills of mankind. The punishments that he inflicted (on those who were ungrateful, those who disbelieved and those who did not pay) never took the form of revenge but of lessons followed by pardon. He politely mystified his patients. A sterile woman asked that she might conceive a child. 'You want nothing more?' the god asked her. 'Nothing more,' the woman replied. She was soon pregnant and remained so for five years. The only wish she had formulated had been granted. She had to return to the sanctuary to ask for a happy delivery, which was immediately granted to her. The child, a healthy boy, according to the inscription which tells the story, ran to bathe at the fountain.

Near the temple of Aesculapius is the long portico where the invalids slept, after purifying themselves with water from the sacred wells, stretched out on the skin of the victim they had sacrificed to the god. A dream came to them which led to their cure. The mysterious *tholos* was reputed to shelter, in the windings of its underground labyrinth, the tomb of the god, who died and was resuscitated. The Doric rotunda, dating from the fourth century BC, decorated inside with beautiful marble Corinthian columns, was the work of an Argive, Polycletus—who must not be confused with his namesake and fellow citizen the great sculptor Polycletus, a century earlier. The same artist, according to Pausanias, also constructed the theatre, the wonder of Epidaurus. Its ample auditorium is visible behind a foreground shaded by pines. But Pausanias was mistaken on this point. It has now been proved that this beautiful building only dates from the third century BC. For one month every year it is filled as of yore with an audience who come from all the towns of Greece to see the Festival productions. Aeschylus, Sophocles and Euripides once again come to life, declaimed in modern Greek by actors from the National Theatre of Athens. In this setting, the tragedies do not seem to be archaeological reconstructions—an effect which the best producers in our theatres are almost never able to eliminate. At Epidaurus the plays appear natural. One feels that the heroes are at home in their surroundings.

The Peloponnese, cut by mountain chains, is a striking example of the partitioning, so characteristic of the Greek landscape, which is sometimes held responsible for the particularism and quarrels of the country. From Nauplia to Sparta the road consists entirely of hairpin bends rising and descending the slopes, broken by long straight stretches across the interior plains of Tripolis and Megalopolis. From the pass which separates Argolis and Arcadia, we turn back for a last look at the Gulf of Nauplia and the Argive plain. A no less splendid panorama greets us, when the valley of the Eurotas suddenly appears, banked by the Parnon and the blue wall of Mount Taygetus, opulent and exuberant, after the sixty-five miles of Arcadia just crossed: olive, orange and lemon groves and vineyards leave not an inch of ground uncultivated.

As Thucydides predicted, Sparta has not bequeathed a single ruin to bear witness to her grandeur. There is not even the evidence of military architecture which would be expected of such a nation of soldiers, because Sparta never desired any other ramparts than the bodies of her citizens. With perfectly straight roads designed by the architects of King Otho, modern Sparta is set in grandiose countryside. We hasten towards Mistra.

Three miles across vineyards, orchards and olive groves, then on a bare peak stands an entire town in ruins, roads bordered with bare walls, windows open to the sky. This is a bombarded town where providence spared the churches. On this spur of Taygetus, Villehardouin constructed his castle in 1249; he had to yield it up to the Greeks ten years later to pay ransom. Originally Frank, Mistra immediately became Byzantine. It was promoted to capital under the despotic regime of Morea, when it enjoyed a brief glory in the empire near its decline. On a white-marble flagstone, marked with an eagle with two heads, in the nave of the Metropolis the last Greek emperor of Byzantium, Constantine Palaeologus, was crowned in 1449. He perished with Constantinople five years later.

In this collection of two thousand dead houses, in the network of roads invaded by wild plants where the buildings, joined by arches, seem to lean on each other for support, the churches, even more than the palace of the despots which dominates the scene, show what Greece could have passed down to the European Renaissance if the course of her history had not been so brutally interrupted. The elegance of their slender proportions, the picturesque walls of freestones separated by bricks—a procedure characteristic of the Byzantine style of the Greek School, the School of Constantinople preferred to use bricks—the play of the arcature, the mullioned windows and the domes, bear witness to a certain taste for the baroque, a relaxation after the severity of classicism which is found again in the thirteenth- and fourteenth-century churches of Salonika. The same state of mind animates the frescoes, dilapidated after long abandonment. Crossing this dead town, one ends up with the same sense of anxiety as in Pompeii or in the ruins of Delos. And it is a pleasure to be greeted by the hospitality of the nuns in the church of Pantanassa and to contemplate, while savouring the local *glyko*, the portico with its light archways, and the festooned dome of this beautiful building which opens like a marvellous loggia on to the living fertility of the plain.

There is a choice of two routes from Sparta to Olympia, either by Arcadia or by Messenia. The first, by way of Tripolis and Vytina passes near Mantinea and Orchomenus and, amidst splendid countryside, crosses the Arcadian mountain range. The second plunges into the impressive canyon of Langada, crosses the Taygetus mountain range and emerges by a deep valley at Kalamata and the fertile plain of Messenia, where fruit and fat black olives are produced. It then climbs again to reach Megalopolis, the homeland of Philopoemen 'the last of the Greeks' who fought ferociously for Greece against the Romans. The small road winds along the foot of Karytaena, with the remains of a Frankish castle on its peak, and reaches Pyrgos and Olympia by Andritsaina, a picturesque mountain town, near the temple of Bassae.

In 1765, a French architect born at Paris, Joachim Baucher, who constructed villas at Corfu and Zante, journeyed to the Peloponnese and was surprised to discover a ruined but entire Greek temple in the heart of the Arcadian mountain range, in a wild remoteness which had assured its safety. All the materials which composed it lay piled at the foot of its columns which were still standing, just as they had fallen one day during an earth tremor. Amidst the chaos of blocks, marble slabs could be seen, with the battle between the Centaurs and the Lapithae sculptured in a continuous frieze. Baucher, architect that he was, immediately understood the importance and the beauty of this building. He realized that he had just discovered a temple forgotten by everyone and which had received no mention since Pausanias described it thus: 'Amongst all the temples of the Peloponnese, it is, after the one at Tegaea, the first in beauty of stone and harmony of proportions.' Tradition attributes it to Ictinos, the architect of the Parthenon. It was consecrated to Apollo Epicourios, the 'Apollo of Timely Aid'. Taken aback by this unexpected discovery, Baucher made a few hasty sketches—today deposited in the Victoria and Albert Museum in London—and returned the following year intending to excavate the building and execute precise surveys. But in the course of that expedition he perished, assassinated by his guides. He had, however, when at Zante, had time to inform the English traveller, Chandler, of his discovery. Chandler was exploring the Near East on behalf of the learned society, the Dilettanti. In 1811, this society organized a scientific expedition to Bassae. Despite innumerable interferences by the Ottoman administration, the temple was excavated in 1812. The Prussian architect, Haller von Hallerstein—whose surveys are deposited in the library at Strasbourg University—thoroughly sketched every block. The slabs of the interior frieze and the sculptured metopes were taken away by mule. Then, not without many underhand dealings—because France tried to buy these precious reliefs—and even brawls on the beach with Turkish police— they set sail for the British Museum.

The temple, which belongs to the Doric order, has a cella decorated inside with Ionic and Corinthian columns. It was begun in about 440 BC and only completed in the first half of the fourth century. The main walls are in the limestone of the country, but the metopes of the pronaos, the Ionic and Corinthian capitals of the interior order, the frieze which surrounds the cella, the tiles and gutters were marble from the Pentelicon. All the marbles which had not been taken to the British Museum perished later on in the lime kilns, in particular the only one of the three Corinthian capitals which had survived, the first to be known in Greek art. The sculptured band of the Ionic frieze ran right round the cella. It borrowed its decoration from the theme already represented on the west fronton of Olympia: the affray between the Centaurs, ill-bred, ribald guests and the people of the Lapithae on the wedding day of Pirithous. The work is not lacking in vigour, the compact muscular forms of the personages betray the chisel of a 'Peloponnesian' artist of the early fourth century. Ennobled by this architectural background, a colossal statue of Apollo in bronze was erected in the cella. At the time when Pausanias passed by, it had already been moved from the temple to the public square of Megalopolis. Behind the cella was a room, containing an interior altar—its existence can be gathered from the marble tiles pierced by an opening for ventilation. Today, despite its ruined condition, the temple, partially restored by the Hellenic Department of Antiquities, is deeply impressive. This results from the lively elegance of its Doric order, the imprint of the beautiful qualities unique to the fifth century, and the magnificence of the countryside which frames it; it is bounded to the south by the summit of Mount Ithome and to the west it looks on to the endless sea.

*
* *

Olympia, like Epidaurus, is a park, but conceived on a scale appropriate to the master of the gods. A late-comer amongst Greek sanctuaries, the reputation of Epidaurus ceased to grow after the end of the fifth century BC and it remained in the second rank. Olympia, on the other hand, after the first Olympiad in 776 BC up to the suppression of the Olympic Games by Theodosius in 383 AD, was the meeting place for athletes and pilgrims from all Greece every four years for over a thousand years. With Delphi and Delos, it is the most captivating of the pan-Hellenic sanctuaries where the consciousness of community of race and civilization was kept alive between the cities, despite bitter quarrels and dispersion in space. When the time of the great games approached, hostilities ceased at the cry of the heralds proclaiming the sacred truce. No army could penetrate the plain of Elis and the pilgrims *en route* for Olympia became inviolable, even if they were on enemy territory. Coming from all quarters of the Mediterranean, Selinos and Cyrene, Byzantium and Rhodes, they crowded in their thousands into the sacred wood of Altis. The motley throng of rich and poor, confident in the clemency of the summer sky, camped in the moonlight around the wall of the sanctuary. The Greeks today do the same when they celebrate a 'panegyric' in one of the isolated chapels, brought to life for one day each year for the feast-day of its saint. The Olympic Games continued for five days, at the full moon, between the end of June and the beginning of September. The nights then are sweet and perfumed. The only people who did not profit from them were the officials lodged in the hostelries near Altis. The provision of food and water for all these men and their mounts, however accustomed they were to making do with little, was beset with problems; their hygiene also. The priests never failed to follow the inaugural sacrifice to Zeus Olympius by a sacrifice to Zeus 'the Fly-Catcher'.

In such a popular sanctuary, piety as well as desire for glory caused the cities and private individuals to honour Zeus by the most varied consecrations: statuettes, bronze goblets, armour or little buildings in the form of chapels. These 'treasures' were lined up on the terrace where each town sheltered the precious offerings of its citizens. No modern museum has anything approaching the richness of the collection of artistic treasures previously locked up in the sacred enclosure of Olympia. Still less the present museum of Olympia, though the tiny part of these marvels collected by German archaeologists is enough to make it one of the most beautiful in Greece. The proximity of work from the most diverse schools was a perpetual incitement to the artists to surpass each other, like the rivalry of the athletes in the stadium. The stadium and the great temple with its marble frontons are symbols of two profound characteristics of the Greek race: the spirit of emulation and the demand for beauty. Sport soon went beyond the immediate necessity of supplying the cities with good soldiers. Each individual wanted to make his body conform to the hidden harmony of the beauty whose image he carried within himself; the artists strove to isolate its laws in order to realize this beauty in statuary. Between the practice of sport and the perfection of Greek art, there is no relationship of cause and effect: both are a reply to the call of the same ideal.

The countryside of Olympia is famous for its gentleness. Wooded hills enclose the horizon; the rocks as soft as clay, cut vertically by torrents, form a striking yellow background behind the dark shapes of the cypresses. In the valley, on the banks of the muddy Alpheus, amidst the laurels and the willows, are the fields where horses and fillies graze, followed by their ungainly colts. The thickly wooded height of Kronion rises at the meeting place of the Alpheus and the Cladeos; between the two rivers and the foot of the mountain, enormous pines hover over the ruins of the Olympic sanctuary, the filtered shade of the undergrowth pierced by rays of sunlight; while the sanctuary itself is invaded by wild grasses and perfumed by irises in springtime. The Peloponnesian stone, the cracked *poros* that was previously brushed over with stucco, does not possess the pure beauty of limestone or marble; earth sticks in its holes, and it gets overgrown with moss and lichens which soon camouflage it amidst the pine needles. The more abstract verticals of the raised columns in the gymnasium and in the temple of Hera are barely distinguishable between the vertical trunks of the trees.

The temple of Zeus and the stadium were the two major buildings of the sanctuary, closely joined in the original when the track of the stadium ran into the square of the temple itself. The athletes then competed in the presence of Zeus, whose marble image rose in the centre of the fronton. A portico called the Echo Portico, added later between the two monuments, destroyed this grandiose plan. The stadium afterwards appeared to be excluded from the sanctuary and was joined to it by a vaulted passage, very shabby despite the Corinthian porch which previously decorated its entrance. Unlike the stadiums at Athens and Delphi, which the munificence of Herodes Atticus provided with stone tiers, the Olympic stadium always remained true to its original simplicity. The course 192·27 metres in length (to be exact, six hundred times the length of Heracles' foot) was edged with banks of grass with room enough for twenty thousand spectators. The banks were enlarged in the course of the centuries by adding new embankments, which each time buried the ex-votos offered to Zeus along the length of the stadium and cleared space for new consecrations. The clearing work going on at the moment by the German School has yielded a rich harvest of bronzes, principally arms. Amongst them the helmet of Miltiades dedicated to Zeus by the great Athenian is a true relic of Greek history.

The temple of Zeus is reduced to a sub-foundation surrounded by a chaos of enormous blocks, fluted tambours, capitals and wide pieces of entablature, in the disorder wrought by the destruction of the Emperor Theodosius at the end of paganism, and the earthquakes which finished it off. There is sufficient material to reconstruct the greater part of the building. But perhaps it is more imposing in a state of ruin, which is to some extent reminiscent of the gigantic piles of the temples of Selinos.

The statue of Zeus in gold and ivory, executed by Phidias, and so monumental that the head of the god, seated on his throne, practically touched the ceiling, has disappeared beyond recall. But still the marvellously sculptured ornaments of the temple remain in the museum, the metopes of the frieze and two marble frontons that the mud of the Cladeos preserved from pillage. On the eastern fronton, two great, calm athletes (Oenomaos, King of Elis, and Pelops), two women in Dorian peplums (the consort of Oenomaos and her daughter Hippodamia), as straight as columns, surround Zeus before the beginning of the chariot race which was to give to victorious Pelops the hand of Hippodamia and the crown of Elis. On the western fronton a terrible quarrel is depicted between the people of the Lapithae and the Centaurs, insolent guests who had attempted to carry off the women of the Lapithae at the end of a wedding feast: rearing paws, lashing fists, tangled bodies, biting and sword thrusts; Apollo towers over the confusion with his fine Olympian countenance.

Still ebullient with its victory over the Medes, the Greek genius felicitously expressed in the naked sculpture of the two frontons, so harmoniously beautiful, the Dorian virtues of male vigour exalted by the Olympic Games. These virtues, spiritualized by Athens, were to lead Greek art to its apogee on the Parthenon.

Smaller but older, the present temple to Hera would seem to have been constructed at about the beginning of the sixth century, with wooden columns and walls of unbaked bricks on a stone base. The wooden columns were, in course of time, replaced by stone columns as one or other of them became worm-eaten. And as the architects were not concerned with standardizing the style of their capitals but every time used the type in use at their period, the peristyle of the temple today presents a curious collection of samples of Greek Doric capitals from the archaic to the Hellenistic period.

When the roofing collapsed in the abandoned sanctuary, the rains eventually soaked the unbaked bricks of the walls so that the clay dissolved and spread in a thick layer over the ruins, miraculously preserving the famous marble Hermes which was found in the very same place that Pausanias saw it. Is it an original by the great sculptor Praxiteles? Is it a skilful Roman copy replacing the work removed by some emperor? Whatever it may be, this ungainly adolescent god, with his ambiguous charm, playing with the child Dionysos, gives a perfect image of beauty as conceived by the master, pleasant, elegant, rhythmic, but not without a certain coldness.

The sculptures from the temple of Zeus are the most beautiful decoration of the Museum of Olympia. But how can one give any idea of its richness in a few lines? More than any of the masterpieces, even those as famous as the Victory of Paeonios, or the well-known pugilist in bronze, more than the abundant collection of bronze statuettes from the geometric period, or of the arms of war consecrated to the god, a small discovery seems to symbolize the historic importance of the museum. It is a simple terra-cotta potsherd, a fragment of a goblet found in the workshop where the great chryselephantine statue was sculptured. An inscription has been engraved with a point on the black varnish of this goblet: '*Pheidiou eimi*', 'I belong to Phidias'.

110

o. Daphni. Le Pantocrator.   110. Daphni. The Pantocrator.   110. Daphni. Der Pantokrator.

111

111. Le canal de Corinthe.   *111. Corinth Canal.*   *111. Der Kanal von Korin*

2. La route de Léchaion
l'Acrocorinthe.

112. The road from Lechaeon
and the Acrocorinth.

112. Straße in Lechaion
und Akrokorinth.

113. *Corinthe.*
Le temple d'Apollon.

113. *Corinth.*
The Temple of Apollo.

113. *Korinth.*
Apollon-Tempel.

114. *Musée de Corinthe.*
Oenochoés corinthiennes.

114. *Museum of Corinth.*
Corinthian oenochoae.

114. *Korinthische Kann*
zum Weingießen im
Museum von Korinth.

5

116

Musée d'Argos.

Museum of Argos.

Museum von Argos.

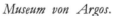

117

118

119

119. Musée National
d'Athènes.
Masque d'or d'un
prince mycénien.
120. Mycènes. La Porte
des Lionnes, le Cercle
des tombes royales et
la Plaine d'Argos.

119. National Museum
of Athens.
Golden mask of a
Mycenaean prince.
120. Mycenae.
Gate of the
Lionesses, the circle
of royal tombs and
the Plain of Argos.

119. Nationalmuseum
Athen.
Goldene Gesichtsmaske
des Fürsten von Mykene.
120. Das Löwentor
von Mykene,
Bezirk der Königsgräber
und die Ebene von Argos.

121-122. *Mycènes. Entrée et*
intérieur du trésor d'Atrée.

121-122. *Mycenae. The Trea*
of Atreus, entrance and inter

122

121-122. *Mykene. « Das Schatzhaus des Artreus »,
Eingang zum Kuppelgrab und Inneres.*

123. *Nauplie. Vue générale.*

123. *Nauplia: general vi*

123. *Nauplia.*

124. *Epidaure. Allée de pins conduisant au théâtre.*

124. *Epidaurus. Avenue of pines leading to the theatre.*

124. *Epidaurus. Piniena. zum Theater.*

-126. Le théâtre d'Epidaure   125-126. The Theatre of Epidaurus   125-126. Theater von Epidaurus
e Festival d'art dramatique.   and the festival of dramatic art.   und Aufführung eines Schauspiels.

127

127. La tholos d'Epidaure:
murs du labyrinthe souterrain.
128. Reconstitution de la tholos
au Musée: l'ordre corinthien.

127. The tholos of Epidaurus:
walls of the underground labyrinth.
128. Reconstruction of the tholos in the
museum: the Corinthian order.

127. Tholos von Epidaurus,
Mauern des unterirdischen Labyrinths.
128. Rekonstruktion des Rundbaus im
Museum: die korinthischen Bauteile.

129

. *Mistra. Intérieur de*
lise de la Pantanassa.

129. Mistra. Interior of the
Church of the Pantanassa.

129. Mistra. Inneres der Kirche
des Pantanassa-Klosters.

130

130. *Vue générale de la cité.*
131-132. *Eglise de la Pantanassa et vallée de l'Eurotas.*

130. *General view of the city.*
131-132. *Church of the Pantanassa and valley of the Eurotas.*

130. *Blick über die Stadt.*
131-132. *Pantanassakirche und das Tal des Eurotas.*

131

132

133

133. *Baie de Navarin.*   133. *Navarino Bay.*   133. *Bucht von Navar*

134

135

34-135. *La forteresse de Méthoni.*   134-135. *The Fortress of Methoni.*   134-135. *Festung von Methoni.*

136

138

139

140

138-139-141-142. *Combat des Grecs et des Amazones.*
140-143. *Combat des Centaures et des Lapithes.*

138-139-141-142.
Battle of the Greeks and Amazons.
140-143. *Battle of the Centaurs and Lapit*

141

142

143

138-139-141-142. Kampf der Griechen und Amazonen.
140-143. Kampf der Kentauren und Lapithen.

144. Olympie et la vallée de l'Alphée.

144. Olympia and the valley of the Alphe

144. Olympia und das Tal des Alphios.

145

145. Olympie. Ruines
du temple de Zeus.

145. Olympia. Ruins of the
Temple of Zeus.

145. Olympia. Ru
des Zeustempels.

146. Olympie. Les colonnes
lu temple d'Héra.

146. Olympia. Columns of
the Temple of Hera.

146. Olympia. Säulen
des Heratempels.

146

147. Olympie. La palestre.   147. Olympia. The palaestra.   147. Olympia. Palästr.

Olympie.
rée du stade.

148. Olympia. Entrance
to the stadium.

148. Olympia. Eingang
zum Stadion.

149

150

151

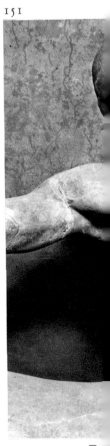

150-151. Détails: femme Lapithe. Centaure.
152. Hermès et Dionysos, de Praxitèle.

150-151. De
152. Hermes

Musée d'Olympie.
*149. Fronton ouest du temple de Zeus.
Apollon arbitrant le combat des Centaures
et des Lapithes.*

Museum of Olympia.
*149. West fronton of the Temple of Zeus:
Apollo judging the battle between the
Centaurs and the Lapithae.*

Museum von Olympia.
*149. Westlicher Ziergiebel des Zeustempels,
Apollon entscheidet den Kampf zwischen
Kentauren und Lapithen.*

152

*pithae woman, Centaur.
nysos of Praxiteles.*

*150-151. Details: Lapithische Frau. Kentaur.
152. Hermes und Dionysos, Werk von Praxiteles.*

153-154. La plage de Killini
et le centre de vacances.

153-154.
The beach at Kyllini
and the holiday centre.

153-154.
Strand von Killini und
Zentrum des Ferienortes.

154

I

III. DELPHI, PHOCIS AND EPIRUS

Between Olympia and Delphi, the Gulf of Corinth is no longer a ditch. It can be crossed in twenty minutes either at Rhion, near Patras, when one would then take the road from Antirhion to Amphissa by the wild mountains of Locris, or at Aegion by the ferry which carries cars and passengers in about three hours to the small port of Itea. Across the plain planted with olive trees, where once the quadriga course ran, the road rises by steep hairpin bends to the promontory of Crysso, still fenced off by prehistoric ramparts, and reaches Delphi, perched on a cliff.

Delphi is certainly the best known and the most visited of all the large Greek sanctuaries. The famous beauty of its countryside even attracts travellers only mildly interested in antiquities. The ruins are ranged on narrow sloping terraces which wide retaining walls prevent from sliding towards the abyss.

Below, there is a cliff two thousand feet deep; above, the luminous screen of the Phedriades rocks, their crest dominating the sea at an altitude of three thousand feet. When one sees Delphi from the road leading to Naupactus, beyond Amphissa, on the Locris Mountains, one is spellbound at the sight of a village on a rock, suspended over space, like white eagles fastened to the wall of the Phedriades. The countryside is impressive, but much less formidable—much less savage—than it is depicted. For someone who has had the chance of knowing Delphi other than as a tourist in a hurry, and of living and working there, the dominant impression, the impression that returns every time in its first freshness, is not of something grandiose but simply of grandeur and calm. The theatre is an excellent observation point at the summit of the sanctuary. At our feet, right at the foot of the ravine, the pebbly bed of the Pleistos can be seen between the olive trees. The grey wall of the Kirphis, flecked by green oak trees, scored by a zigzagging mule-track, rises opposite. In the morning, the sun rising on Arakhova throws hollow shadows on the sides of the mountain, powdered with a light bluish mist. In the evening, the sun hits directly the great reflector of the Phedriades, forming red flames and justifying the name given the rocks by the ancient peoples—Phlemboukos—meaning 'flaming'. It is then perhaps that the Olympic serenity of Delphi is at its best. The depth of the silence can be measured when it is disturbed by the sonorous braying of an ass, the impact of an axe on stones, the muffled crackling of a thousand hoofs as a troop of goats pass on the road. This countryside has been described too frequently as Dantesque, almost infernal, in order to make it accord with the false and conventional image of a prophetic pytoness, foaming at the mouth in hysterical delirium. This is not so. Despite the broken relief there is nothing tragic in the scenery. It is wonderfully suited to be the dwelling place of a

E

sun-god, who was also the god of philosophers and mathematicians. The overwhelming impression is of a perpetual, luminous enchantment which, far from startling the mind, leads it on to contemplation. One can envisage the companions of Plutarch, seated on the steps of the temple opposite the valley, interrupting their dialogue to remain silent with their thoughts.

For fifteen centuries, this unchanging framework was all that remained to Delphi of its past. Deprived of its illustrious name, the 'Navel of the World' became a hamlet of three hundred hearths, Kastri, where the sad grey houses had not even the whitewash that the villages of Attica and the Cyclades throw over their poverty like the cloak of Noah. Practically none of the antique monuments had emerged except for some rows of bricks from the western portico, as red as the Phedriades, and the great polygonal wall which the centuries had not been able to bury completely. In the fields under the olive groves, scattered sarcophagi served as water-troughs for the flocks, and occasionally rocky vaults had opened up in the side of the mountain. But history guarded the memory of the treasures which had disappeared, and then the archaeologists came.

A few blows of a pickaxe at the foot of the polygonal wall during exploratory excavations undertaken by the French School of Athens in 1863 brought to light several hundred inscriptions, the porch with marble columns consecrated by the Athenians and the sphinx of Naxos, one of the principal works of Greek sculpture of the archaic epoch. The prospect was encouraging. The French government voted an extraordinary credit for the pursuit of research. The Emperor Napoleon III doubled the figure out of his personal purse, and decided that a warship should land the archaeologists in the port of Itea to enhance the prestige of the expedition. The political vicissitudes of Greece and France made this fine project fail. It was resumed on a larger scale in 1892 after laborious negotiations—which at times reached the extreme limits of courtesy—between French archaeologists and their German and American colleagues. The village covered the exact site of the antique sanctuary; France expropriated the lot. However, the residents would not lightheartedly leave a site where their ancestors had lived for more than thirty centuries. The effort was made to console them by explaining that the new village had a much more beautiful view over the Bay of Itea. They replied that it was much more exposed to the wind. It was not without reason that the Delphians, fourteen centuries before Christ, had installed themselves in the hollow of this sheltered and sunny theatre. Despite difficulties, excavation began. The first Decauville tip-waggons, decked with the Greek and French colours, carried the debris to the Pleistos— under police protection. The feelings of the Delphians have greatly changed since. The grandeur of the work accomplished has effaced the memory of the sacrifice involved. Seventy years of continuous effort by the French School of Athens, assisted by the Delphians themselves, have stripped Delphi of its rags.

Today, as of yore, pilgrims from all corners of the world follow the road to Castalia.

When we knew Delphi in 1949, the civil war was at its height. It was then a frontier post, surrounded by barbed wire, within reach of the Andartes hidden on Parnassus. Every evening all the men quartered in the ruins of the Fine Arts School went on guard behind the network of electric bulbs, which at night outlined a luminous no-man's land all round the village. If an ass, forgotten in the darkness, rubbed itself against the barbed wire, it immediately released a volley of brisk, random fire from the watchers, to which the Andartes perched on the summit of the Phedriades would reply. No great damage was done to anybody, while the echoes of the Pleistos amplified the rumbling of machine-gun fire mixed with the frightened braying of the donkey.

What a contrast today! Delphi has become terribly 'touristy'. A vast avenue, lit up in the evening, now leads to the village. Along the main road, hotels and taverns have increased, as well as stalls selling pseudo-Greek vases, carpets from Arakhova, *tagari* or striped bags and the olive-wood *bastouni* with a wide wooden hook at the end to enable the shepherd to catch his sheep by their paws. But if you climb the steep roads cut to the whim of winter torrents, you come to the village of Parnassus, leading its own mountain existence, indifferent to the cohorts of de luxe coaches and chromium taxis. Around the ambitious unfinished church, the houses of whitewashed clay have geraniums and fragrant basil growing in old tins painted with lime on their unguarded balconies. Black goats with horns shaped like lyres, and asses laden with red and black blankets and carrying their masters' lunch in striped *tagari*, come to drink cool water under the arches of the fountain. Then they go to the fields, either under the olive groves watered by the Fountain of Castalia or on the scorched hills of Arakhova where vines are grown to produce the *kokinelli* of Delphi, a pale-pink wine with a sweet taste and a resinous smell. From the top of the village one can see, across the roofs of rust-coloured tiles, Itea, the port of Delphi, in the depths of a bay sown with islands and against the spectacular background of the Peloponnesian mountains. Apollo sailed from the port, escorted by Cretan sailors, to dispute the 'rocky Pytho' which he wished to make his own domain, with the old goddess Earth. A forest of olive trees, green or blue according to the time of day, stretches out along the narrow gorge of the Pleistos, scales the sides of Parnassus below Delphi and spreads out towards Amphissa in the plain, where chariot races were once held. In the west the view is blocked by the chaotic summits of the Locris Mountains, where trails of snow often remain till the end of spring.

The chapel of St Elijah surrounded by a small cemetery is built on an antique terrace on a rocky spur, which separates the village from the ruins. The Amphictyons, delegated by the Greek people to watch over the fortunes of the sanctuary, probably sat there. Near by, there are circular flagged threshing-floors. In the summer when the mules yoked in fours turn round over the grain, the winds act as winnowers on this crest where the ancients had raised an altar to them.

Once clear of the spur, the site of ancient Delphi, in its entirety, a vast theatre opening on the Pleistos, comes into sight. Why was it established there? Because of the abundant springs bubbling up from the rocks—the 'Kerna' and the Fountain of Castalia; because of the road which, winding its way between Parnassus and the Helicon, joins the Gulf of Corinth to the rich plain of Thessaly. But how did it become the home of the gods? Legend replies that two eagles, similar to those still hovering interminably over the ruins, were released by Zeus at each extremity of the world. They met at Delphi: 'Navel of the World'. The spot is very precisely marked by a sacred stone, the *omphalos*. Legend also says that the goats of Parnassus were seized with madness when they approached a certain crevasse filled with strange fumes. When the shepherds, intrigued by this phenomenon, came to smell the crevasse, they fell victim to a delirium which gave them a view of the future but sometimes landed them at the bottom of the gulf. To avoid this danger while still retaining the advantages of the gift of prophecy, they installed a woman on an iron support across the fault in the rock. This was the first Pythia on the first tripod. It is also told that the old goddess Earth was the first to occupy the sanctuary, that she was guarded by the serpent Python, and that she uttered oracles through the mouth of the Sibyl, 'the Delphica', represented by Michelangelo on the ceiling of the Sistine Chapel. Apollo came to rob her of her domain and had in his turn to defend it against the claims of Heracles. This celebrated dispute was represented by an anonymous sculptor on one of the frontons of the Treasury of Siphnos. The gods are shown, each pulling the prophetic tripod towards himself while Athena, in the role of a reasonable sister, tries to restore peace.

Pilgrims coming from Boeotia, like the valuable Pausanias himself, came first to the sanctuary of Athena Pronaia, stretching the full length of a narrow terrace amidst olive trees. Today the spot is called Marmaria, 'the marbles', because the ruined buildings unfortunately served as a quarry and worse still as nourishment for the lime kilns. Sculptured blocks from the *tholos* have been retrieved even in the walls of the houses of Amphissa.

Despite this vandalism, the monuments of Marmaria still offer a veritable abridged history of Greek architecture. There are, firstly, the very ancient capitals, flat as pancakes, which are the sole remains of the older temple of Athena. They lie on the foundations of the second temple in *poros*, built in the sixth century BC to replace the former one. Enormous rocks falling from the Phedriades in 1905 completed the ruin of this second building, but on the much abused temple a corner column remains standing, miraculously complete, covered with a fine layer of stucco, its capital, with the swelling quarter-round, as alive and supple as a human muscle. The anonymous Doric treasury represents the elegant and severe architecture of the fifth century. It symbolizes the stylistic transition from the old *poros* temple to the geometric precision of the two beautiful 'expiatory temples' of the fourth century, offered to Athena by the Delphians following a battle which stained her sanctuary with blood. The first is a Doric temple in limestone of St Elijah; the cut of the stone is a marvel of precision. The six columns of its façade are doubled by four interior Ionic columns. The second is the *tholos*, a Doric rotunda in marble. Its svelte and shiny columns rising in front of the cracked walls of the Phedriades, ivory amidst the twisted trunks of the olive trees, contrast their calculated diagrammatic beauty with the accidental beauties which frame them. Corinthian columns, amongst the oldest known, decorate the interior of the building, precious incunabula of a style which was later so successful with the Romans and after, with our own architecture.

The Ionic order is represented at Marmaria by a notable monument of the sixth century BC: the marble Treasury of Marseilles. When the Phocaean colonists settled on the coast of Provence the nations trading in the country, the Ligurians and the Carthaginians, were not pleased by the arrival of new competitors. The Marseilles fleet had to do battle one day with the Corsicans in the open sea. The adversaries retired, both so sorely tried that an objective observer would have found it difficult to decide which had won. The men of Marseilles, convinced that the victor was perforce the side which thanked the gods for victory, bestowed the title upon themselves by constructing in honour of Athena—and at Delphi so that all could see—a charming Ionic building with palmiform capitals decorated with an illuminated frieze. Of this, there remains the pedestal, with a wide fluted torus surmounted by a delicate astragal. The marble is carved so carefully that one's hand automatically moves to caress the polished epiderm.

An abrupt path leads from Marmaria to the gymnasium. Athletes from all corners of the Greek world trained there before Pythian competitions under a large covered porch as long as the stadium. After the exercise, they found changing and assembly rooms grouped around a peristyled courtyard. They could refresh themselves in the cold swimming pool, fed by the waters of the Castalian fountain. The spring bubbles out of the rocks very near the fault which like a sabre thrust separates the two Phedriades. A veritable symbol of Delphi, it provided the water necessary for purification and for the maintenance of the temple. To exorcise this pagan concept, a small chapel was built to St John the Hunter above the fountain; it figures in old engravings but has left no trace except the imprint of its apse buried in the rock.

The terraces of the principal sanctuary, enclosed by a rectangular wall, are spread out below the wall of the Phedriades. In the centre there is the massive pedestal of the polygonal wall which encloses the terrace of the temple. At the summit there is the fan of the theatre. Towards the foot, at the first turning in the Sacred Way, stands a brilliant marble dado: the treasure of the Athenians. The Sacred Way winds amidst jumbled stones, brightened in March by bunches of almond trees. After one crosses the surrounding wall, there is on the right the pedestal of the bronze bull offered by the Corcyrians; on the left stands the site of the Athenian base where sixteen bronze statues commemorated the victory of Marathon. Conquerors of Athens, the Spartans took great pains to erect thirty-seven bronze statues of their gods and their admirals just outside the city. Humiliated in its turn, Sparta saw the bronze statues offered to the gods by its Arcadian victors rise up in front of its own monuments. Before you have gone more than a few steps along the Sacred Way, with Pausanias' book in your hand, you can already enumerate nearly one hundred bronze statues that crowded along the roadside. Nothing illustrates better what a pan-Hellenic sanctuary such as Delphi meant to the Greeks. In the first place they were marvellous centres of propaganda, where the cities were all the more anxious to demonstrate their piety as these demonstrations proclaimed to all their glory, their power and their wealth. Then they were excellent museums, schools of fine arts where the rivalry of the cities aroused the spirit of competition in the artists, permanent exhibitions which improved the taste of the discerning public. On simple pedestals along the Sacred Way, hidden in the treasuries, crowning the crests of walls or perched on high columns, hundreds of statues were piled up in the packed sanctuary, thanking the god for services rendered, good business, fortunate enterprises, victories of Greek over barbarian but also, unfortunately, of Greek over Greek. The donors were the cities or individuals, kings such as Croesus, or prosperous courtiers. Of marble and bronze, precious wood, gold and ivory, these innumerable ex-votos, masterpieces mixed with the mediocre products of industrial art, disappeared bit by bit, melted down to finance wars, carried off by the emperors of Rome and Byzantium and later burned in the lime kilns of Kastri. Those saved by protective burial are today sheltered in the museum.

The Sacred Way rises slowly towards the temple, turns at the height of the Treasury of the Athenians, reconstructed stone by stone by the French School from 1904 to 1906, and skirts the great polygonal wall. It is amazing to see the arabesques formed by the capricious joints of the bricks. It is curious to think how such a puzzle was assembled, its pieces often weighing more than a ton. Many hundred inscriptions are engraved on the surface, mostly acts of emancipation. A slave was able to buy back his liberty from his master, if the latter agreed, and this purchase had to be guaranteed by an official act. But a slave, simply a 'masculine body' or a 'feminine body', as bereft of legal personality as a goat or a mule, could not be party to a contract of sale. Hellenic astuteness solved the problem by the following expedient: the slave gave his savings to the priest of Apollo who was supposed to buy him back from his master on the god's account. Divine property, the slave was henceforth sheltered from all new slavery. The act of sale was then engraved on the stone. Over a million such acts were made at Delphi over several centuries. The conditions attached to them offer the historian of ancient law and economics a collection of documents unique of its kind.

In front of the polygonal wall there are three white columns, the Portico of the Athenians. Its wooden entablature sheltered a curious trophy, the enormous flaxen cables which joined the bridge of boats thrown by Xerxes over the Hellespont, 'like a yoke on the neck of the sea'. Let us greet, as we pass through this assembly, the most subtle monument—the Treasury of Cyrene which materialized mathematical abstractions in space—and the most glorious monument, the pedestal of the golden tripod borne by three bronze serpents consecrated by the Greeks after the communal victory over the Persians at Plataea. Beyond the great altar of Chios, we find ourselves in front of the temple of Apollo reconstructed in the fourth century BC. The beautiful limestone blocks clamped with iron have been dislocated by landslides, by pillagers of metal and treasure-seekers. Despite the fact that some tambours of columns have been replaced in the façade since 1940, a serious effort is needed to imagine the original size of the building, almost as large as the Parthenon, where the famous maxims were engraved on two statues of Hermes: 'Know thyself' and 'Nothing in excess'.

Pilgrims have crowded the esplanade of the temple throughout the centuries, anxious to know the future. How did the ceremony proceed? A goat was led before the temple and was sprinkled with water. If the animal shivered, the god agreed to the sacrifice and consented to a consultation. If the animal did not react, it meant that the god refused to speak and misfortune came to anyone who passed beyond. The only Pythia who ever braved the divine wish left the temple bereft of reason.

Once the preliminary sacrifice had been made and the tax paid, the consultants were introduced into the temple, first those whom the Delphians, in recognition of some service, honoured with a *promantie*, that is to say, permanent priority. In the most secret sanctuary, in the *adyton* the Pythia, a Delphian of canonical age, officiated. At the time of Plutarch she was generally a poor peasant whose ignorance guaranteed her docility to divine inspiration. Seated on the tripod, behind a curtain which hid her from sight, the prophetess inspired by Apollo proffered inarticulate sounds which the priest translated on a tablet. It was a sibylline translation which gave the god the glory of successes and made it possible to impute failures to the foolishness of the consultants. In the archaic epoch cities and kings questioned the Pythia on the most serious matters of state. But at the time of the Medean wars, it must unfortunately be admitted that Apollo himself did not remain insensible to the seductions of Persian gold and, in the end, the powerful men of the day attempted to inflect the voice in the sense most favourable to their own interests. The cities then pursued their political life without the oracle but did not cease to add to the wealth of the sanctuary by innumerable offerings to the god.

Lodged in a recess in a corner of the sacred enclosure, the theatre dominates the whole of the field of ruins. From its tiers, the beauty of the light playing on the valley can be appreciated. Constructed to hold five thousand spectators, it has no place at all amongst the largest theatres of Greece but it is one of the best preserved. Its acoustic qualities are reinforced by the natural sonorousness of the countryside. The ancient dramas are still played there before the most beautiful background imaginable for the verses of the Greek tragedies. More than one spectator can recall the performance of *Prometheus* by Aeschylus where, as if in reply to the invocation of the leader of the chorus: 'Appear, eagles of Zeus', the griffon vultures of Parnassus, by a striking coincidence, began to hover in the sky.

Higher still, the track of the stadium spreads out behind a curtain of pines, a quiet haven to relax in, after the rather rough climb, watching the antics on the scorching stones of the large green lizards with red tongues or the familiar grey birds, the Sitta of the rocks, with black beaks and red feet, which fill the sanctuary with their song.

Beyond the stadium, a path climbs towards Parnassus. Without being an athletic exploit, the ascent demands time and a good guide. However, it is well worth the trouble. At first very arid, the path soon reaches an area covered with pines and cedars, cut by fields where flocks graze guarded by shepherds with voluminous hairy cloaks and, most important, by those veritable wild beasts— the dogs of Parnassus—trained to combat wolves. The Corycian cave opens under a cliff, where the Bacchantes of Delphi, the Thyiads, honoured Dionysos with mad winter races in the mountains. From the summit, when the sky is clear, the view embraces nearly all Greece, from Taygetus to Olympus, from Euboea to the Locris Mountains. With a good deal of luck, you can even point out the grey of Athos, emerging from an uncertain horizon where sky and sea mingle.

The Museum of Delphi can compete with the Acropolis Museum in the richness of its collection of pre-classical sculpture. Most of it consists of decoration from the entablature or frontons of buildings: metopes from the small monopteros of Sicyon, possibly constructed by the tyrant Clisthenos to shelter in the sanctuary his chariot which had been victorious at the races and consecrated to the god; rare but precious flotsam from the frieze of the Marseilles treasury; wonderful friezes and a fronton from the marble treasury which the inhabitants of Siphnos consecrated to Apollo from the revenue from the gold mines, providentially discovered and shortly afterwards, submerged beneath the waves. Here are the marble *couroi* and *corai*, gleaming with youth. Standing on the principal fronton of the archaic temple rebuilt by the Alcmeonides, they commemorated the period when the Athenians, leading the quadriga of the god, hacked a way for him through the hitherto inviolate forests, the sacred way which led him to Delphi. The marble metopes of the Treasury of the Athenians, probably erected between 490 and 480 to commemorate the victory of Marathon, at the time when the archaic period came to an end seem to have been designed to express all its qualities of vigour and charm: this is evident in the muscular elegance of the bodies, the decorative and graphic style of the clothing, smiles animating the faces, in life and in death itself.

The Naxian sphinx, with graceful sickle wings, has crossed the centuries so discreetly, seated like a stylite at the top of its high column, that no ancient author thought it proper to mention it. On the other hand, well before excavations brought them to light, we knew that the Argives had consecrated the statues of the two brothers Cleobis and Biton at Delphi, the good-humoured athletes with heavy plaited wigs who now welcome visitors opposite the door of the museum. Herodotus relates how these two sons of a priestess of Hero one day harnessed themselves to their mother's chariot in a procession in place of a team of oxen who were late in arriving. Touched by this mark of filial piety, the mother prayed to the goddess to grant her children 'the best that could happen to mortals'. That evening, the two youths went to sleep and never awoke. Divine benevolence spared them the knowledge of the decadence of the body and the disillusions of life which are the old age of the soul. Such is the fundamental pessimism of a people whose art seems a hymn to the zest of being human, to the joy of bodies flowering in beauty.

The waggoner, clothed in green bronze, holding the reins of a phantom team, the flexible athletes of Scopas raising their pathetic eyes to the empty sky, the dancers of Delphi, hymned by Debussy, who follow their solemn dance up to the top of their acanthus column, Antinous also, the favourite of Hadrian, with the sulky face of a spoiled street arab—they all symbolize the continuity of the offerings which flowed to the 'Navel of the World' until the end of paganism. They are an infinitesimal part of what was once its decoration! According to the phrase coined by a historian of Delphi: 'We have only collected the small change of a fabulous fortune.'

Some eleven miles from the sanctuary, the road from Livadia to Delphi divides in two; the left fork leads to the village of Distomo. At this cross-roads, Oedipus, returning one day from Delphi met a traveller on his way there, got into a quarrel with him and killed him. He was to discover much later that he had unwittingly committed patricide, thus fulfilling the first part of the terrible Delphic prophecy, according to which he would kill his father and marry his mother.

The monastery of St Luke or Hosios Loukas is easily reached by way of the road from Distomo. For a long time the poor state of the roads kept it in the same hermit-like solitude as it was at the time when Luke the Stiriote settled in this valley of Mount Helicon to devote himself to God, far from the dramas and brutalities of the tragic tenth century. Tossed hither and thither by the wave of invasions, he finally retired to the valley, which the monastery overlooks today, a peaceful and charming spot, with green shade and ever-fresh water.

What a strange personality this monk was! Illiterate, rustic, pushed from retreat to retreat by his bitter desire for solitude, he was, like the ascetics of his period, exclusively preoccupied with faith and salvation. But his piety bore no resemblance to the sombre passion which ordinarily possessed the rough Byzantine anchorites. Luke, according to the anonymous author of his 'Life', loved flowers, dreamed by the banks of the water and, in his infinite tenderness for all nature, conversed with the birds, the deer and the snakes by the wayside. It was as though the Muses, the ancient mistresses of Mount Helicon, had decided to slip a touch of poetry into his contemplative soul to give to the East the St Francis it lacked. He prophesied. He also cured. When he died in 951, his fame had gone beyond the boundaries of his little hermitage. In mid-winter, by paths covered with snow, the peasants of Phocis came to receive his last benedictions. The tomb of the saint, near the small church of Santa Barbara, perpetuated his miraculous qualities as healer and soon a convent and a church were erected near by.

The present church, which has replaced these primitive buildings, was erected in the first half of the eleventh century by the Emperor Basil, the 'Killer of the Bulgars'. With the Nea Moni at Chios and the church at Daphni, it is one of the only three eleventh-century Byzantine churches in Greece which have preserved an important part of their mosaic decoration. Charles Diehl, whose studies contributed to rescue this beautiful building from oblivion, declared that 'it is not only the elegance of the forms and the felicitous proportions of its plan and the skill of its construction which make it comparable to the most beautiful buildings of Constantinople. The rich marble decoration which lines the inner walls, the numerous mosaics which cover the outer walls and the arches, make it one of the most interesting and most complete monuments bequeathed by Byzantine art.'

Side by side with a smaller church consecrated to the Virgin, the principal church bears its high cupola on a tambour with sixteen faces, itself standing on a square plan. The walls are built of heavy blocks, mostly borrowed from the ruins of the ancient city of Stiris. Their sober decoration of serrated bricks, projecting pillars, and clamping in free stones, emphasizes the internal anatomy of the building. Brightened by numerous columned windows joined by sculptured chancel slabs, the walls balance the enormous thrusts of the cupola, effortlessly and joyfully. Light, the symbol of truth and salvation, penetrates the nave in waves, illuminates the large polychrome slabs of the paving, makes the marbles of the walls iridescent and the gold of the mosaics shimmer. The Pantocrator who dominated the church, as at Daphni, disappeared in the collapse of the cupola during an earth tremor in 1593. But the crown of apostles at the base of the dome still exists, symbolizing 'the descent of the Holy Ghost at the very place where the mystery of the Eucharist took place'. The Platytera Madonna is enthroned in the apse on an unreal golden ground. The Annunciation—now destroyed—the Nativity, the Presentation at the Temple, the Baptism figured in the pendentives. The narthex is decorated with scenes from the Passion and the Resurrection, including the famous descent into Limbo inspired by the apocryphal Gospel of Nicodemus. Amongst the numerous figures of madonnas and saints which decorate the groined vaults, the gynaeceum and the soffit of the arches, the portrait of Luke the Stiriote to whom the church was dedicated is particularly worthy of notice. Frescoes complete the decoration in the western chapels and in the crypt. The completely Attic grace of Daphni must be forgotten here: compact, thick-set, with heavy heads and awkward gestures, bundled up in stiffly pleated clothing, the personages of Hosios Loukas seem rustic at first glance. But an unmistakable sense of the monumental in composition and the delicacy of the colouring contradict this first impression and express the personality of a school of painting which Chatzidakis defines in these terms: 'The school of painting which realizes the ideal of this tradition (Byzantine) at the monastery of St Luke, in the first years of the eleventh century, with a plenitude of expressive motifs that were not seen again, could not be a regional or purely monastic school. The mosaics of St Sophia at Kiev, works of Greek painters of the same period and the same tendency, bear witness to the vast radiance of this artistic tradition in the Byzantine world and in the zone of its influence.'

*
* *

The mountain range of Parnassus can only be crossed at its two extremities, to the east by the beautiful road from Athens passing the Arakhova pass; to the west, by the mediocre Brallos road which skirts the savage Locris Mountains. This road was driven in 1917 by the French Territorials in order to supply the Salonika Expeditionary Corps by land, avoiding the Aegean Sea which was infested with enemy submarines. The road emerges at the western extremity of the depression which prolongs the Boeotian plain, immediately climbs the slopes of Callidromos and crosses the valley of the Spercheios at Lamia. In passing, we pay our respects to the memory of the Pass of Thermopylae. Today, Xerxes would find the narrow goat path replaced by the motorway which leads straight to Athens across Boeotia. Skirting the mountain of Othrys, we reach Larissa, in a plain surrounded by high peaks, Othrys in the south, Ossa and Pelion in the east, Olympus in the north and in the west the barrier of the Pindus. We are in the heart of Thessaly, the country of the Centaurs, the native land of Aesculapius. This immense plain is the domain of storks and also of sheep, grazing in large flocks, guarded by nomad tribes. We are already in the steppes, watered by the Peneus. The river rises in the forests of Pindus, waters the Meteors in passing, where in days gone by it cut fantastic menhirs in the rock, and finishes in all its beauty in the Aegean, by the celebrated valley of Tempe, under a tangle of willows and plane trees scented by jasmine and terebinth.

A visit to the Meteors has lost in picturesqueness what it has gained in comfort. A road now leads to most of the monasteries, perched on their gigantic cippi. It threads its way between the strange black peaks scarred with cracks and faults which give them an other-worldly look. Sometimes, an abrupt path or a stairway hollowed in the rock, sinuous and steep, joins the road to the monasteries. The monks who built them in the troubles of the fourteenth century wanted to make them inaccessible except by vertiginous ladders down the face of the rocks. The highest-placed used a net hoist. The old wooden winch is still on show at the Great Meteor—hanging down over fifty yards of nothingness. It once hauled up visitors and provisions, driven against the rock by the least breath of wind. Now there only remain a small number of monks, sometimes only one, in a large deserted convent, suspended between heaven and earth. They offer their guests the traditional *glyko*, a spoonful of jam accompanied by an *ouzo* and a glass of fresh water. This is consumed on the wooden balconies opposite the valley, the view blocked in the distance by the hazy mountain chain of the Pindus.

After the Meteors, the road continues westwards, following the course of the Peneus. It crosses the Pindus at a height of nearly five and a half thousand feet at the Metsovo pass, in a countryside of forests, of deep and savage valleys different from the conventional Greek countryside. Even in March, snow-ploughs have to clear a passage in snow-drifts six feet thick, and packs of wolves wander through the undergrowth. The village of Metsovo is inhabited by the strange Wallachian population, who are probably ancient Illyrians latinized. Their dialect is actually connected with the Romance languages. Mainly nomads, they spend the summer with their flocks on the Pindus; in the winter they descend towards Epirus and the Ionian coast or towards Thessaly. They are tall, with very intelligent blue eyes. Many of the leaders in the War of Independence were Wallachian. The people of Metsovo still wear the old costume: a tunic of blue serge, white stockings and a round toque for the men; red and black tunics with wide sleeves for the women. But unfortunately this race is dying out.

From Metsovo, the Arachtos valley leads down to Janina, a romantic city full of memories of Ali of Tebelen, with its fortress and its two minarets mirrored in the lake. 'Napoleon is emperor, and I am nothing. But . . . .' Thus quoth the pasha of Janina in his sumptuous residence overlooking the lake in the presence of an imperial envoy. Master of one of the most prosperous fiefs of the Ottoman Empire undermined by anarchy, he knew how to use this to his own advantage. He was born in 1744 in the Albanian village of Tebelen, the son of minor notables. He set his sights high. His moral observations having led him to the conclusion that Beauty, Goodness and Good could only be identical with the interests of Ali, he was able with clear conscience first to make himself a 'Haidoute' or ring-leader, before he was named Dervendji-Bachi, or commissioner of roads, charged with the precise task of liquidating the 'Haidoutes', a task which he accomplished magnificently. A pasha who had once saved him from the gallows and whom he himself had incited to revolt he ordered to be strangled for rebellion. The pasha who had taken him as his son-in-law suffered the same fate. He brought to their senses and to the tomb some pretentious souls who had thought it their vocation to be pashas. He put the Greeks of Souli to the sword though he had promised to settle them elsewhere if they submitted and left their mountains. He allied himself to the English when the French held Corfu, to the French when the English replaced them there. As his horror of a vacuum made him at once fill himself the vacancies he had created, he rapidly became one of the best endowed of all the pashas of the empire and Janina, his capital, the most prosperous town in Greece. It made large profits from leather and skins, from the cereals it sold to Corfu and the neighbouring islands. Cotton and silk were woven there. Its embroideries were renowned, as were its colleges where Greek, Latin and French were taught. The unfortunate Pouqueville spent nine years there, by order of the emperor as French representative, passing from favour to the cruellest insults, according to whether the pasha needed France or was antagonistic to France.

Ali Pasha nursed the dream of appropriating Greece for himself as a hereditary fief, as Mohamet Ali, another Greek-born ambitious man, did in Egypt. Facing a weak power, he was energetic. He opposed a mixed army from impregnable citadels. He possessed a fabulous war treasure. He would undoubtedly have triumphed over the Ottoman troops who united against him in 1821 if the arms which he had used so well to raise himself had not contributed to precipitating his fall. This great corrupter saw his partisans corrupted. His two sons, bought by the sultan, surrendered the key citadels which were in their keeping. 'Alas! Poor Ali,' he wept. 'You have only begotten chickens!' This liar was, in his turn, the victim of a lie. Putting his faith in a promise which guaranteed him life, pardon and liberty, he went to the little island of St Pantaleimon, in the middle of the lake, to negotiate the symbolic surrender of the citadel. When the citadel had surrendered, Ali was put to death. Aged seventy-seven, he defended himself to the last, like the old lion he was, and had time before he expired to have the wife he cherished strangled so that she should escape enemy outrages. He had to be dragged across the floor of the retreat where he had taken shelter before he could be brought down. His head, properly stuffed, was hastened to Constantinople and exposed on the battlements of the Seraglio between those of his two sons whose betrayal had not been long to their advantage. The powerful pasha of Janina was buried in two pieces, his body at Janina, his head at Constantinople, under a marble cippus that can still be seen at the cemetery of the Silivri gateway. He died in the same year as the Greek uprising—the Greeks whom he had not been afraid to favour in order to embarrass the sultan—to avenge the massacres of Souli and to put an end to a colonization which may sometimes have been picturesque, but was also tyrannical and barbarous.

About thirteen miles south of Janina, in a deep valley at the foot of Mount Tomatos, are the ruins of one of the oldest oracles of Greece. Zeus prophesied at Dodona through the voices of the oak trees. The excavations of the Hellenic Archaeological Society have revealed an imposing theatre next to a stadium and amongst various buildings, the remains of the *manteion* where the oracles were delivered. The prophets of the god, who walked with bare feet in order to remain in contact with the inspirational current which came from the ground, interpreted the flight of the doves, the murmur of the water, dice or the sonorousness of a large bronze basin which the statue of a child, moved by the wind, struck with its whip. But more than anything else, they foretold from the voice of Zeus which they heard in the murmur of the sacred oak. Placed apart from the theatre, one of the largest in Greece, the monuments are badly damaged by the rough climate of 'Dodona of the two winters'. The blocks of limestone are crumbling under the effects of frost and necessitate costly upkeep. Although the antiquity of the oracle was venerable and its reputation widespread as far as Lydia, its remote position in a mountain range prevented it from enjoying a prosperity comparable to that of the sanctuary of Delphi perched on its luminous rock beside a much frequented maritime route.

IV. SALONIKA, ATHOS, THASOS AND SAMOTHRACE

SALONIKA is the second city of Greece and was the first during the decadence of Athens. With Ravenna and Constantinople, it possesses one of the most beautiful collections of Byzantine monuments in existence. In the past, despite its treasures, it remained rather on the margin of the tourist movement. Today, it is the first to receive the wave of cars coming from Yugoslavia. The new road which runs along the Thermaicus Gulf at the foot of Olympus and the straits of Euboea, to the north of Boeotia, now joins the capital of the north to the capital of Greece through wonderful coastal countryside. After the war, Salonika, the natural port of the Balkans, might have perished of suffocation, cut off from the nations whose maritime traffic it assured. But it turned resolutely towards other activities: an oil refinery and a large steel works helped to develop the industrial character of a city which had, till then, been mercantile and agricultural. The considerable tourist trade contributes to a prosperity shown in the vast and beautiful avenues recently opened and the large blocks of flats on the outskirts which replace the dusty suburbs of yesteryear. From the slopes of Mount Khortiatis, far from the tumult of the new quarters, a whole network of calm streets suddenly appears, edged by old timber-framed houses. Their projecting storeys supported by painted brackets, their roofs protruding in wide weather-boards, seem to be trying to prevent the freshness, the shade, one might almost say the mystery which goes to make up the charm of these old districts, from escaping to the sky above. Here and there, gardens provide a touch of green, and rose-coloured brick churches emerge from blocks of tumbledown cottages. A marble plaque near a door marks the birth-place of Kemal Ataturk. A decapitated minaret, the circle of the ramparts against which the renewed wave of invaders beat—everything here speaks to the memory in the language of a brilliant past. From the height of the acropolis, the bay is visible, fifteen miles deep, and on the right on a clear day the blue pyramid of Olympus can be seen. A few caiques and an occasional steamer land in the vast port which once welcomed vessels from all points of the Mediterranean, when Byzantine Salonika could call itself the second capital of the greatest empire then existing.

A late-comer amongst Greek cities, it was founded in 315 BC by the King of Macedonia, Cassander, who called it after his wife Thessalonika—changed by us into Salonika. The splendid gilded bronze vase, the mixing bowl with the Bacchantes, discovered in a tomb near the city, at the place called Dherveni, dates from this period. A neighbouring tomb contains a few leaves of oxidized papyrus, remains of the oldest Greek book that we possess. The excellence of its anchorage and its position on the trade route from Dyrrachium to Byzantium, which joined Italy to the Asian provinces, favoured the expansion of the city in Roman times. It received Cicero when he was exiled and sheltered the second church founded by St Paul on European soil. There are few traces of this ancient period. The monumental history of the town begins in the fourth century.

In order better to resist barbarian pressure on the frontiers of the empire in the Danube region, the Emperor Galerius established himself at Salonika. He erected in a then uninhabited area a palace, a triumphal arch which still spans the Via Egnatia, and finally joined the palace by a long gallery, now destroyed, to a mausoleum which the Christians transformed into the church of St George in the fifth or seventh century. This vast rotunda, still flanked by a minaret which bears witness to its vicissitudes, is certainly one of the major monuments of Salonika. The size of its interior space strikes one at the entrance, and the rhythmic simplicity of the doors which once opened on to a circular gallery and now, walled in, have become alcoves.

The gold of the mosaics glistens in the semi-darkness. The oldest, dating from the fifth century, with their patterns of flowers and birds arranged above the niches, are reminiscent of luxurious embroidery on some Eastern stuff. The dome was decorated in the seventh century. Under a golden sky which symbolizes the ineffable splendours of the beyond, in front of a background of fantastic architecture inspired by the art of the Antioch mosaics, the saints of the primitive Eastern Church are shown in prayer, each with his name and the date of his feast-day inscribed at his side. Doubtless, it is less beautiful than the mosaics of Ravenna and does not possess their happy equilibrium, but this sumptuous calendar nevertheless occupies an equally important position in the history of early Christian art.

Galerius' stay at Thessalonika was marked by violent persecutions of the Christians. One of his victims was a certain Demetrius, an obscure character who was to become strikingly famous at Salonika. Arrested for preaching the faith, he was incarcerated in a Roman bath near the stadium, then, by the emperor's command, executed by spear thrusts. The martyr was buried secretly and soon the whereabouts of his burial-place was forgotten. But at the places where he was tortured, miracles were not slow to multiply. In the year 412, Leontios, a prefect of Illyricum, who had been cured by the saint, erected a large basilica on the site of the stadium and of the Roman bath which had been his prison. However, he left the monumental fountain, the nymphaeum, which was preserved under the apse of the new church. A miracle soon happened: a perfumed balm began to pour forth inexhaustibly from the antique fountain—a miraculous oil, distilled, it was thought, from the tomb of the saint—who could no longer be anywhere but underneath the basilica. From emperors to beggars, crowds flocked there. St Demetrius became the patron, the defende

156

155. Naupacte. La forteresse.   155. Naupactus: the fortress.   155. Naupacte. Die Festung.
156. Le ferry-boat d'Itéa.   156. The ferry-boat at Itea.   156. Das Dampfschiff von Itea.
157. Femme d'Arachova.   157. Woman from Arakhova.   157. Frau aus Arachova.

157

158. Delphes. La basse vallée du Pleistos et la baie d'Itea.   *158. Delphi. The low valley of*

leistos and the Bay of Itea.   *158. Delphi. Die Niederung des Pleistos und die Bucht von Itea.*

159. Delphes.
Le sanctuaire d'Apollon.

159. Delphi.
The Sanctuary of Apollo.

159

159. Delphi.
Heiligtum des Apollon.

*160. Delphes. La
tholos de Marmaria.*

*160. Delphi. The tholos
of Marmaria.*

*160. Delphi. T[
von Marmaria.*

161. Delphes. Le trésor des Athéniens et le portique des Athéniens devant le mur polygonal.
162. Décret honorifique gravé sur le mur du trésor.

161. Delphi. The Treasury of the Athenians and the Portico of the Athenians in front of the polygonal wall.
162. Honorific decree engraved on the wall of the Treasury.

161. Delphi. Schatzhaus und Säulenhalle der Athener vor der polygonalen Mauer.
162. Grausame Verfügung an der Mauer des Schatzhauses.

163

163. Delphes. Le temple
d'Apollon et les Phaedriades.

163. Delphi. The Temple of
Apollo and the Phaedriades.

163. Delphi. Apollon-Tem
und die Phaedriaden.

4. Delphes. Le théâtre.   164. Delphi. The Theatre.   164. Delphi. Theater.

*165. Delphes. Représentation
au théâtre antique.*

*165. Delphi. Production
in the ancient theatre.*

*165. Delphi. Vorführ[...]
des antiken Theaters.*

6. Delphes. Le stade.   *166. Delphi: the stadium.*   *166. Delphi. Stadion.*

167. Dispute du trépied entre Apollon et Héraclès.   *167. Contest for the tripod between*

168. Assemblée des dieux.   *168. Gathering of the gods.*   *168. Versammlung der Götter.*

169. Enlèvement des   *169. Kidnapping of the*   *169. Entführung der Töchter*
filles de Leucippe.   *daughters of Leucippus.*   *des Leukipp.*

167-171.
Musée de Delphes.
Trésor de Siphnos.

Museum of Delphi.
Treasury of Siphnos.

Museum von Delphi.
Schatzhaus
der Siphnier.

Apollo and Hercules.   *167. Disput über den Dreifuß zwischen Apollon und Herakles.*

170

171

170-171. Combat des dieux et des géants.   *170-171. Battle between the gods and the giants.*   *170-171. Kampf der Götter und Giganten.*

172. Trésor de Sicyone:
razzia des Dioscures.

172. Treasury of Sicyon:
raid of the Dioscuri.

172. Schatzhaus von
Sikyon:
Raubzug der Dioskuren.

172-177.
Musée de Delphes.
Museum of Delphi
Museum von Delph

172

173

173. Cléobis et Biton.   173. Cleobis and Biton.   173. Kleobis und Bit

. Le Sphinx des Naxiens.   174. Sphinx of Naxos.   174. Sphinx von Naxos.

175

175. *L'Aurige.* 176. *Antinoüs.* 177. *Colonne des Thyiades.* 175. *The Charioteer.* 176. *Antino*

176

177

7. *Column of the Dancing Girls.*   *175. Wagenlenker   176. Antinous.   177. Säule der Thyiaden. von Delphi.*

178

178. *Monastère d'Hosios Loukas.*
Mosaïques d'Hosios Loukas:
179. *La Pentecôte et la Vierge et l'Enfant.*
180. *La Nativité.* 181. *Le Baptême du Christ.*

178-181.
Monastery at Hosios Loukas.
Mosaics from Hosios Loukas.

178-181.
Kloster Hosios Luka
Kuppelmosaik des
Klosters Hosios Luk.

182.   Le Lion de Chéronée.   *182. The Lion of Chaeronea.*   *182. Der Löwe von Chärone*

. Les Météores.   183. The Meteors.   183. Die Meteore.

183

184

184. Les Météores.
Le monastère de Varlaam.

184. The Meteors.
Monastery of Barlaam.

184. Meteora-Klo
von Varlaam.

*Météores.
monastère
Roussanon.
. Le théâtre
Dodone.*

*Meteors:
nastery of
ssanon.*

*Theatre
Dodona.*

*eora-Kloster
Roussanon.
. Theater
Dodone.*

*187. Corfou. Ilot de Pondikonisi.   187. Corfu. Islet of Pondikonissi.   187. Korfu. Das Inselchen
Pondikonissi.*

of Thessalonika, and his church one of the most famous of Christianity, with
St Sophia of Constantinople and the Holy Sepulchre at Jerusalem. Damaged by
fire for the first time in the seventh century, it narrowly escaped destruction in
the great fire which reduced half the town to smoke in 1917: an irreparable
disaster, of which forty years' patient labour have attempted to limit the
consequences. On October 26, 1948, the feast-day of St Demetrius, the restored
church was solemnly returned to the faith.

It is a vast basilica cut by a transept and divided into five naves by four
rows of columns in cipolin and in green marble from Thessaly. Each row
supports a second row of smaller columns on wide arches. Beneath the roofing
of the central nave a series of imposts enlivens the bareness of the walls, today
devoid of the polychrome marbles which once adorned them. All that remains
of the interior decoration is the marble capitals of the lower colonnade—
amongst the most beautiful that Byzantine architects have bequeathed to us—
and some of the mosaics presented to the saint by private individuals. These
followed each other on the walls of the side-aisles without any preconceived
plan and bear witness to the piety of the faithful. One represents St Demetrius
amongst the children entrusted to his care. Another shows the patron saint of
the city standing between the bishop and the prefect Leontios whom he is
holding informally by the shoulder. His body seems to form a rampart before
the city's walls, their crenellations visible in the background. The stiffness of
the garments and their long folds, sumptuous and immobile, are in vivid
contrast to the liveliness of the faces. That of the saint is imprinted with celestial
youth, while the men are bearded, wrinkled and bearing the traces of the
accidents of mortal humanity, yet full of a serene dignity.

The fifth century also saw the construction at Salonika of a church called
Eskijuma by the Turks, and Haghia Paraskevi or church of the 'Acheiropitos'
by the Greeks because it sheltered a miraculous icon, 'not made by the hand of
man'. The earth around it has risen above the former level. The roof of the
central nave, crudely repaired in the course of centuries, is now lower than
before. Thus the original proportions have been gravely impaired. None the
less, entering this great basilica with three naves, bathed in light from two rows
of windows with marble mullions, it is easy to understand why Byzantium
considered it one of the three most beautiful basilicas of the town, with St
Demetrius and St Sophia. Today, it is the oldest basilica on Greek soil, although
long neglect has unfortunately resulted in the loss of its marbles and mosaics.
Even so, deep-blue fluted vases with long branches bearing fruit, flowers and
birds emerging are still distinguishable against a background of burnished gold
in the curve of the arcades which join the pillars. A charming baptistery has
recently been revealed beneath a block of slum houses which had made even
the memory of its existence disappear.

The construction of St Demetrius and the Acheiropitos bore witness to a prosperity likely to arouse a great deal of envy. Theodosius the Second thought it prudent to build a rampart round the town. With the aid of St Demetrius, Slav attacks against the city were repelled at the end of the sixth century, and Salonika was free to develop and flourish. It became the second city of the empire after Constantinople, when Alexandria and Antioch fell into Arab hands. It reorganized its municipal institutions, and opened the routes of central Europe to its commerce. Following the movement of its merchants, two missionary brothers, Cyril and Methodius, went to evangelize the Slavs. This spirit of enterprise, this boldness, also showed in architecture. In the seventh century, the church of St Sophia was built. Here, the first attempt was made to adapt the dome of oriental origin to the traditional type of basilica. It is not difficult for technicians to criticize certain clumsinesses in the design, betraying the architects' perplexity at the new problems posed by the adaptation. But to the unsophisticated visitor, with its dome borne on powerful arcades supported by four thick fluted pillars, and the Madonna of mosaic aureoled with gold, glittering in the domed roof of the apse—added after the disputes of the period of iconoclasm—it is full of grandeur. A Christ in Glory stands on the dome surrounded by the Virgin and by the twelve apostles. This work probably dates from the middle of the eleventh century.

This brilliant period ended in tragedy. Blinded by its own magnificence, Salonika remained oblivious of the dangers threatening it. It grew soft with opulence. It neglected its ramparts. On July 29, 904, the black-sailed fleet of the Saracens commanded by Leon of Tripoli appeared in the roads and catastrophe was inevitable. St Demetrius himself remained deaf to the pleas of a city degraded by its own luxury. The next day, the garrison surrendered. For ten days hideous carnage prevailed which did not even spare the churches. Then the enemy withdrew, carrying off twenty-two thousand prisoners.

Despite this disaster, despite repeated invasions by the Bulgarians, Salonika once again enjoyed a true renaissance in the tenth and eleventh centuries, thanks to the firm policy of Roman the Second and the Emperor Basil, known as the Killer of the Bulgarians. The chroniclers compared the city to Constantinople and praised the splendour of its annual international fair. The jewel of Byzantine architecture in Salonika dates from this period—the charming church of Our Lady of the Blacksmiths, consecrated by a high official, his wife and his three children. Even today, the neighbouring streets still resound with the hammer blows of copper artisans forging large basins for baptismal fonts, pitchers, and homely cooking pans, and moulding the feet of candelabra.

After the fumblings evident in the construction of St Sophia or the church of Hosios David (although the latter is a more skilled erection), Our Lady of the Blacksmiths appears to be a perfect success and the crowning point of a long series of experiments. It was the type of church built in the shape of a Greek cross to which Byzantine architects were henceforth to remain faithful.

As distinct from the large primitive basilicas which were adorned primarily in the interior, this is already a work of art from outside, with the delicate tints of its brick-coloured walls, discreetly ornamented with 'saw-tooth' motifs and with columns set in the corners, crowned by a display of curved and triangular frontons, of domes and arched windows. Its very approach is a delight. The spectator pronounces it exquisite but then realizes that the adjective only renders the freshness of a first impression without taking account of the classical austerity of the sober decoration. In the interior, the frescoes have suffered a great deal from overpainting by the Turks. The central dome, the image of the firmament, shows Christ rising in the heavens surrounded by the Virgin, the angels and the apostles. In the apse the Virgin stands and prays between the Archangels Michael and Gabriel. The principal episodes in the life of Christ unfold on the other vaults. Experts see the influence of the school at that time flourishing in Constantinople in both the architecture and the style of the frescoes. Our Lady of the Blacksmiths is one of its most finished works.

Salonika then underwent all the dramas that shook the Byzantine Empire. In the twelfth century, the city was occupied for several months by the Normans whose atrocities surpassed those of the Saracens in horror. The historian of this dark period was Eusthates, deacon of St Sophia and a commentator on Homer and Pindar. In the thirteenth century when the Crusaders, the masters of Constantinople, shared the spoils of its empire, Salonika fell to Boniface of Montferrat. It became the capital of a short-lived Latin kingdom and the Provençal or Perigordian poetry of the troubadours Raimbaud de Vacqueyras and Elias Cairel was heard in the court of the new king. Liberated from foreign overlordship in 1222, Salonika was for a time the capital of an independent empire. Then it acknowledged the authority of Constantinople, liberated in 1261, and remained under its sway until the era of Turkish domination.

In the thirteenth century the church of St Catherine was built and in the fourteenth that of the Holy Apostles. St Catherine's is a veritable triumph for modern archaeology. It was converted into a mosque and, whitewashed and disfigured by chance accretions, no longer gave any indication of its delicate perfection until the patient and careful work of restoration re-created its original purity. Like Our Lady of the Blacksmiths it is a church in the shape of a Greek cross, rounded off by a gallery on three sides. On the exterior, there is the same extraordinary display of curved frontons, of thin colonnettes at the corners with slender drums which support the domes with their scalloped edges. In the interior, two unknown painters have depicted with a sure hand the miracles of Christ, the Communion of the Saints, and the great teachers of the Eastern Church.

The church of the Holy Apostles seems to be the highest achievement of Byzantine art at Salonika before the final collapse. Surrounded by trees, it stands erect in the old city and the silhouette of its five domes raised on octagonal drums, flanked by slender colonnettes, charms from afar. In design it resembles St Catherine's. The style is the same, but here the tendency to the baroque is even more accentuated. The exterior of the walls is adorned with all the motifs obtainable from ingenious combinations of bricks. The architect has shown skill less in conceiving this multiplicity of lozenges, Greek borders, tracery and chevrons, than in integrating them harmoniously and lucidly into one architectural composition.

Rich mosaics have been found in the interior, valuable as much for their art as for their documentary value. In the fourteenth century, the use of the fresco, which was less of an expense than the mosaic, had spread almost everywhere in an impoverished empire. Mosaics of this epoch are rare. The Pantocrator Christ stands on the dome, surrounded by prophets; on the pendentives there are the four Evangelists, and elsewhere one finds the customary episodes from the lives of Christ and the Virgin.

Salonika, 'City of the Graces', was now near its end. Dynastic quarrels, social and religious disputes prepared the way for its fall into the hands of the Turks, who already surrounded it on all sides, in Macedonia and in Thessaly. The city tried to save itself by selling itself to the Venetians. The attempt was in vain. An inscription engraved on a column of the Acheiropitos, the old basilica, can still be read today: 'The Sultan Murad took Salonika in the year 883 of the Hegira.' Such was the epitaph of Byzantine Salonika.

The city was none the less preserved from decline by the natural advantages of its position. Under the Turks, it remained what tradition had made it—the port of the Balkans. Its decimated Greek population was increased by an influx of foreigners to form an extraordinary hotch-potch of peoples. In the fifteenth century a strong contingent of Jews from Spain, thrown out by the Inquisition, was added. Minarets grew higher than Byzantine domes. Athens had become a village but Salonika still looked a capital. The city was at the heart of the Balkan problem and, in 1908, saw the birth of the revolt of the Young Turks. In 1912 it welcomed the Greek troops and regained its liberty on the very day of the feast of St Demetrius. In 1916, Venizelos formed his revolutionary pro-Allied government in Salonika. The Anglo-French army disembarked there in 1917, leaving behind the large cemeteries which surround the city. In the same year, a fire broke out devastating more than two hundred acres of houses and making seventy-two thousand people destitute. The French architect, Hebrard, contributed to the reconstruction of the destroyed areas according to a town-planning design that provided for the future. Today, therefore, Salonika consists of an old town with the charm of Constantinople side by side with a modern metropolis. In 1922, ninety-seven thousand refugees from Asia Minor came to replace twenty thousand Turks sent back to Turkey. The considerable Jewish community, well established since the sixteenth century, was annihilated during the last war. Thus history, whose vicissitudes gave

Salonika the most motley population that ever was, has finally restored its racial unity. The Greeks, who were almost a minority in 1908, now make up the whole population of the city (in 1961, 373,635 inhabitants). They are energetic and active, with liberal or advanced political traditions. The University of Salonika teaches in the language of the people (*demotiki*) while the University of Athens insists that its teachers and students use the 'purified' language (*katarevousa*). The symbol of the spirit of enterprise of the great city is its annual fair which occupies a whole district in the east of the city, not far from the elegant modern museum where the treasures of its past are now displayed.

*
* *

One must leave Salonika by boat in the morning and see the strange silhouette of Athos emerging against the sky in the haze of the sea. It looks like a pyramid rising from the waves—more than six thousand feet high and moored to the mainland by a slender isthmus. Athos is the most easterly of the three capes of Chalcidice that stretch out into the Aegean like a hand with three fingers. It encloses the vast gulf which bathes the islands of Thasos and Samothrace. Ancient navigators only knew it because of its evil reputation. King Xerxes preferred to try to cut the isthmus by canal in 480 BC, rather than sail his fleet round this inhospitable rock where, lashed by the winds, the vessels of his father Darius came to grief in 490, and thus saved Greece.

This historic event would not have been enough to give Athos the fame it was later to enjoy. But in the tenth century AD certain pious men chose to lead a life of asceticism there either as hermits or in small communities, because it seemed hardly to be a part of the rest of the world. It was then that the monk Athanasius, later known as the Athonite, arrived amongst them (in 1963 it was exactly a thousand years ago). He belonged to a rich family of Trebizond. Orphaned when very young, his relatives brought him up in the capital, Constantinople, and when he entered holy orders his high connections gave every reason for anticipating a brilliant career. But the austerity of his soul urged him to Athos. He lived at first as an anchorite in a cave. Then, prepared for his task by this harsh retreat, he founded the first of the great monasteries, the Grand Lavra, with the support of the Emperor Nicephorous Phocas. The rule of the Grand Lavra, taken from that of the Constantinople monastery of St John of the Stoudion, laid down a cenobitic, i.e., an absolutely communal way of life, whether meals, sleep, duties or even clothes were concerned. Vegetables and fish, oil and black bread formed the usual diet, which never contained meat. In the year 1000, Athanasius died in the church that he had constructed. He was crushed by the collapse of the dome. But following the example of the Grand Lavra, three new monasteries had been established on the eastern coast—Iviron, Vatopedi and Philotheos. These four venerable foundations were followed by many others from the eleventh to the fourteenth centuries. Finally, the high walls and crenellated tower of Stavroniketas were erected in the sixteenth century, amidst the woods, overlooking the sea. It is the last in date of the monasteries, making a total of about forty which formed, in the period of their prosperity, the theocratic republic of Athos, the Hagion Oros or Holy Mountain.

This republic, today numbering no more than about two thousand members, used to contain about forty thousand, recruited from all the countries where the Greek Orthodox Church held sway. Greeks from Greece and Asia Minor lived side by side with Serbs and Bulgarians, grouped for preference in the convent of Chilandari, with the Macedonian Bulgars of the convent of Zographou and with Russians from St Pantaleimon or Russiko. A bull decreed by the Emperor Constantine Monomakh in 1060, which is still in force, forbade entry to the Holy Mountain to every 'woman, to any female, to any child, to any eunuch, to any smooth visage'. This prohibition was applied literally. There were neither cows nor she-goats nor hens among the domestic fauna of Athos! Novices in black robes (*rasoforos*), monks of the little robe (*microskimos*) and monks of the large robe wearing the attributes of Christ, skull and crossbones embroidered in white (*megaloskimos*)—all the inhabitants of Athos had to let their beards grow and even their hair, which they gathered together in a chignon tucked under their black bonnet or *scoufia*.

Endowed by emperors and wealthy private individuals, this republic experienced a period of prosperity which led to a certain relaxation in its way of life. The facilities of the 'idiorhythmic' régime were preferred to the rigours of the cenobitic régime imposed by Athanasius. The former allowed a certain minimum of individual life, acknowledged the right to property, relaxed the ascetic rule and permitted the consumption of meat, on condition, however, that it was cooked outside the monastery. The discretionary authority of an omnipotent abbot appointed for life was replaced by the more understanding administration of two *epitropoi* assisted by a changing council. Since then, the convents of Athos have been divided between Cenobites and Idiorhythms. The latter are usually the wealthier members, and the history of Athos falls into periods of relaxation favouring the development of the Idiorhythms, followed by periods of austerity demanding a return to the cenobitic routine. Both disciplines are in force today.

Although the Holy Mountain officially forms part of the Greek state which is represented by a governor and a detachment of gendarmerie, it is largely autonomous. In its administrative capital of Karyes lying amidst the freshness of orchards irrigated by running water, the twenty members of the holy community (one delegate from each convent) and the executive commission of the four epistates (of which each possesses one-quarter of the seal which must authenticate decrees) administer the affairs of the peninsula. Nowadays, these affairs are much reduced in scale since the Russian revolution in 1917, revolutions in central Europe and confiscations by the Greek state have deprived the convents of vast landed properties, the source of their wealth, and also cut to a large extent donations and new members. There are now twenty convents, but many are almost empty and are slowly being overwhelmed by a poverty which the present occupants are unable to stem.

The relative autonomy of the Holy Mountain is still evident in the formalities which the male tourist must undergo before he may enter. Once he has obtained the authorization of the Greek Ministry of Foreign Affairs and a letter of introduction from the Archbishop of Athens, he must request the *diamonitirion* at the Holy Epistasia of Karyes. This is his permit to stay in the convents. On its presentation, the *archondari*—the monk whose duty it is to take charge of visitors—will dispense as generous a hospitality in his monastery as discipline will permit. It will always begin, as everywhere in Greece, with the traditional *glyko*. If the visitor is of note, the bells or the *simandres*, long rods of wood or iron that are struck with a mallet to summon the religious to service, will ring out at his arrival.

The monasteries of Athos were established in the neighbourhood of the coast, leaving the inaccessible uplands of the interior to the anchorites and the small detached communities, known as *skites*. Iviron, Vatopedi, Karakallou, Russiko, Xenophontos, are actually on the sea coast. But the visitor must sometimes walk for more than an hour from his point of disembarkation to reach St Paul or Simopetra perched on wild cliffs, or the Grand Lavra, Docheiariou, Chilandari, Stavroniketas, Xeropotamu, sheltered on the side of hills and in the midst of woods. The monasteries are linked together by muletracks which disappear in places beneath the tall grass and brushwood. They climb along the sides of the mountains to skirt the towering cliffs. Then suddenly one has a bird's-eye view, amidst the trees, of a monastery withdrawn in the depths of a creek, its boat drawn up on the dry sands.

Weather permitting, the quickest and easiest communications are by sea. Each monastery has its boat and its little harbour was defended, at a time when piracy was rife, by small forts or turrets of which fine specimens are visible at the Grand Lavra, Karakallou and Iviron.

It is impossible to describe these monasteries one by one. Each has a marked individuality as a result of its position in the countryside and its architecture. The superimposed arcades of Zographou, its church and its red-and-white striped tower are buried deep in the woods. Seen from afar, Vatopedi resembles a fortified town beneath roofs of mossy shale amongst which the sombre red of its church bursts forth. Russiko is even more impressive for its massive effect than it is pleasing for the unexpected charm of its Russian style, with its bulbous domes of green bronze, its sparkling gilt crosses, its immense white façade and its large expanse of bricks and mortar. St Paul is surrounded by a Dantesque décor. Light balconies hung dizzily over nothingness on the high walls of Simopetra look like scaffolding which aerial plasterers have forgotten to take down. But despite their diversity the monasteries of Athos conform to a common design.

The nucleus is the church, the *katholikon*, which is isolated in the midst of the main courtyard. It is usually in the shape of a Greek cross but with the addition of an apse at each end of the transept. The interior of the walls is covered by frescoes arranged according to the canons of Byzantine painting. The screen which separates the nave from the Holy of Holies is in gilded wood, sculptured and richly decorated with icons. It mingles its brilliance with that of an enormous circular candelabrum in copper, suspended by chains from the vault of the central dome. As in all Orthodox churches, the visitor receives an impression of mystery, of richness, of confusion and of suffocation in this glittering half-light perfumed with incense.

The monastery proper surrounds the church that it overlooks. It turns to the world the hostile walls of a fortress, dominated by a crenellated tower that is both belfry and library. Only oriel windows in the Turkish manner and a few balconies relieve the military appearance with a touch of fantasy. Usually, a well-defended narrow gateway leads to the square tower around which the various buildings, with their floors of cells or arcaded walks, are grouped. The guest apartments are situated on the most open sides. In the courtyard of the monastery there is also the *phiale*, fountain or sacred well, covered by a dome resting on columns. The *phiale* of the Grand Lavra is justly famous. It stands near a majestic cypress and its splendid porphyry basin is surrounded by eight columns surmounted by Turkish capitals with stalactite decoration and joined together by older sculptured marble plaques, that appear to date from the tenth century. The rooms of the monastery are blessed with holy water from the *phiale* on the first day of every month and on the anniversary of the baptism of Christ.

The Grand Lavra also provides the most curious example of the refectory (*trapeza*), which sometimes stands on its own in the courtyard, between the church and the *phiale*, and is sometimes incorporated in the buildings that surround it. The refectory of the Grand Lavra is decorated with paintings and is noteworthy for its marble tables, each intended to seat ten monks. The kitchen is generally a vaulted hall pierced in the centre by a chimney beneath which is the hearth. The system is primitive and is partly responsible for the fires that ravaged the monasteries.

For wars, decrepitude, fires and poverty have spared only a few of these ancient monuments. Only the churches of the Protaton at Karyes and the Grand Lavra and Vatopedi date as far back as the tenth century. The principal part of the church of Chilandari dates from the thirteenth century. But on the whole, few of the buildings are older than the sixteenth century and most of the

188

189

188-189. Mosaïques de Pella.
Scène de chasse au lion. Dionysos.

188-189. Mosaics from Pella:
a lion hunt ; Dionysos.

188-189. Mosaike von Pella.
Löwenjagd. Dionysos.

190

191

190-191. Salonique. Vue générale et quai Vasiléos Constantinou. *190-191. Salonika. General view and the Quay of Vasileos Constantinou.* *190-191. Blick auf Saloniki un das Vasileus Constantin Ufer.*

192

193

92-193. Salonique. L'exposition   192-193. Salonika. International   192-193. Internationale Ausstellung
ternationale. La Tour Blanche.   exhibition. The White Tower.   in Saloniki. Der weiße Turm.

196

Salonique.
194. Cratère de Dherveni.
195. Arc de Galère.
*196. Saint Georges. Rotonde romaine
successivement église et mosquée.*

Salonika.
194. Urn from Dherveni.
195. Galerius' Arch.
*196. Saint George: Roman rotunda,
successively church and mosque.*

Saloniki.
194. Krater aus Dherveni.
195. Galeriusbogen.
*196. St. Georg, Romanischer Rundbau,
nacheinander Kirche und Moschee.*

198

197

97. *Mosaïque de l'église
aint-Georges.*
98. *Mosaïque de la basilique
t-Démétrius: Saint Démétrius
t deux enfants.*
99. *Coupole de l'église Sainte-Sophie:*
*Pantocrator entouré de la Vierge
rante, de deux anges et des apôtres.*

197. *Mosaic from the Church
of St George.*
198. *Mosaic from the Basilica of
St Demetrius: St Demetrius
and two children.*
199. *Dome of the Church of
St Sophia: the Pantocrator
surrounded by the worshipping
Virgin, two angels and the
Apostles.*

197. *Mosaike in St. Georg.*
198. *Mosaik der Demetrius
Basilika: Hl. Demetrius
mit zwei Kindern.*
199. *Kuppel der Sophienkirche,
Pantokrator, umringt von
der anbetenden Jungfrau
zwei Engeln und den Aposteln.*

200

Salonique.
200. Basilique Saint-Démétrius.
201. Eglise Sainte-Catherine.

Salonika.
200. Basilica of St Demetrius.
201. Church of St Catherine.

Saloniki.
200. Basilika des Hl. Demetriu.
201. Kirche der Hl. Katharina.

203

204

204. *Mont Athos.*
Monastère de Vatopédi.

204. *Mount Athos.*
Monastery of Vatopedi.

204. *Berg At*
Kloster Vatop

monasteries were reconstructed between the seventeenth and nineteenth centuries. None the less some icons and collections of precious manuscripts bear witness to their age and past wealth. Today, the monasteries succeed in surviving by the work of their monks who cultivate the ground or carve wooden bric-à-brac for the benefit of visitors. But their poverty does not detract from the warmth of the welcome they reserve for visitors and it is this above all that unites the Holy Mountain to the rest of Greece. With the beauty of its changing countryside, the strangeness of the survival of this theocratic republic of men in our epoch, the picturesqueness of its great sea-girt monasteries, Athos offers the visitor a unique spectacle in Europe, the memory of which will never fade.

Not far from Athos, bastion of Greek Christianity, there exists in Macedonia and most particularly in the neighbourhood of the towns of Salonika, Verria, Drama and Serrai, an extraordinary survival of an old pagan cult assimilated by the new religion, the feast of Anastenaria and its Fire Dances.

It is celebrated every year on May 21, the feast-day of St Helena and St Constantine, by a religious sect whose members are known as Anastenarides. These are recruited particularly from Greeks repatriated from Bulgaria when there was an exchange of minorities. The title is hereditary but the brotherhood can accept new members after appropriate initiation. During the year, the Anastenarides function as magicians and healers. But their supernatural powers show more particularly on May 21.

The celebrations are prepared long in advance. On May 2, as soon as night has fallen, they march amidst great ceremony to a sacred fountain. All this while they hold aloft the images of St Helena and St Constantine whom they adopted as patron saints when they were converted to Christianity. They purify themselves in the fountain, throw several pieces of money into the water, light torches and carry back the images in procession to the church. On May 20 an enormous pyre is heaped up on the town square while the Anastenarides lead a young bull adorned with flowers in procession near the church. The next day, May 21, after mass, the leader of the sect makes the sign of the cross over the animal with an icon hung with bells to ward off evil spirits. He then kills it, taking care that its blood gushes on to the wall of the church. He then divides the flesh and skin amongst all the inhabitants of the village and leads his followers to the meeting place of the sect. In an atmosphere of stifling heat, surrounded by the smoke of incense, before the images of St Helena and St Constantine, they all prepare for the ordeal of the night by dancing until they are out of breath, emitting hoarse shouts to the feverish sound of musical instruments. Then, when night falls, plunged in ecstasy, they make their way to the village square where the bonfire is ablaze. Each of the Anastenarides, holding the icons, performs a mystic dance on the embers, barefoot, without suffering the slightest injury. The Orthodox Church prohibited this ceremony for a long time but now tolerates it, the most impressive of the numerous survivals which link present-day Greece, through Christianity, to its most distant past.

*
* *

The road from Salonika to Cavalla travels through about one hundred miles of varied countryside. It runs along the edge first of the two lakes, Coronia and Volvi, then of the Gulf of Thrace, crosses the muddy course of the Strymon at Amphipolis under the good-natured gaze of the colossal marble lion, the cousin of the lion of Chaeronea, which surmounted the summit of a monumental tomb in the fourth century BC. It then plunges into a long and sinuous valley at the foot of Mount Pangaeus where Philip of Macedon used the gold mines to buy many consciences and to assure his empire in Greece. This prince founded a town to which he gave his own name, Philippi, on the site of the little hamlet of Crenides on the edge of a fertile plain, now planted with tobacco.

Apart from the ancient theatre and the foundations of a temple, very little remains of the Macedonian city. The interest of Philippi lies in its vast forum and particularly in its Byzantine monuments, explored by the French School of Athens and the Hellenic Archaeological Society. In actual fact Philippi occupies an eminent place in the history of the evangelization of Europe. The Apostle Paul and his disciple, Silas, coming from Alexandria of Troas, landed at Neapolis, today Cavalla, and stopped at Philippi, an important stop on the famous Via Egnatia which joined Italy to the provinces of Asia. Paul and Silas, according to Acts, first converted a trader in purple dyes named Lydia who was the first Christian to be baptized on European soil—in 51 AD. Their second recruit was a slave, a pythoness whom they exorcized. But once the demon who inspired her had been driven away, she also lost her prophetic gifts. The owners of the slave, who had reaped profits from her, incited the population against the two apostles. Dragged to the public square, they were beaten with rods and then thrown into prison, Roman citizens though they were. Despite these tribulations, the first Christian church of the West was founded. Four basilicas in the fifth and sixth centuries were to give evidence of its vitality.

A rocky spur separates Philippi from Cavalla, the tobacco capital. Its picturesque promontory appears suddenly between the pines. The arcades of the aqueduct, the chimneys and cupolas of the monastery founded by Mohamet Ali stand out against the white of its houses. Recently, large-scale works have created a whole modern and flowery district along the edge of the port. The new museum is situated here. In the rear of the bay, sixteen miles out to sea, the massive silhouette of Thasos stands out.

Together with Corfu, Thasos is the only Greek island where the car driver can comfortably take his car. Two ferries make the crossing in forty-five minutes between the lagoon of Keramoti, water-melon centre of Greece, and the principal town of the island, also called Thasos. The island is entirely composed of a broken mountainous mass with four crests rising over three thousand feet. Mount Hypsarion overlooks the sea from its three thousand seven hundred feet. The slopes covered with forests of pines, plane trees and oaks, fall abruptly to the eastern coast, cut by rocky coves and bays fringed with deserted beaches. The translucent waters shimmer against a background of white-marble or gneiss pebbles streaked with silver. In the south of the island, in the Bay of Haliki, the marble quarries, dazzling in the sunlight, look like sumptuous swimming pools beneath the level of the water. The roads which are still rough and ready lead to the picturesque villages of the interior, Panaghia with its great plane trees, Theologo, which was the capital at a time when piracy made the coast deserted. Taken all in all, Thasos, refreshed in summer by the breath of the Meltem, was endowed with a tourist potential which new travel conditions in Greece have only recently enabled it to exploit. Hotels have multiplied in the town where Greek and foreign summer visitors rub shoulders during the season. The vast beach of Makri-Ammo, previously solitary, is now bordered by the buildings of a motel perched on a slope in the pines. Most charming of all the tourists are the bees which arrive in whole swarms every summer from the arid mainland to spend their holidays in the meadows of the island, amongst the thyme, lavender, origanum and a thousand varieties of flowers.

Plunged for long in depression, the island has awoken. It has resumed exploitation of its iron mines and marble quarries and the rough raw blocks of marble, scored by the smooth channels of the miner's bar, are sent to Germany and Italy. It sells wood from its forests, fruit and honey and it is beginning to enjoy a prosperity which it has not known since antiquity.

Except for the pirates and various invaders, Thasos had no visitors for a long time other than archaeologists. During the fifteenth century, Cyriacus of Ancona described it when it was in Genoese ownership. The French archaeologist, Miller, charged with a scholarly mission by the Emperor Napoleon III, made some soundings and took the three beautiful pre-classical reliefs representing Hermes, Apollo and the Muses to the Louvre. In 1912, the French School of Athens undertook the systematic exploration of the island and brought to light, in addition to the marble surrounding wall with its sculptured doors, the theatre backing on to the mountain, under the pines, facing a wonderful view over the gulf and the town, the sanctuaries of Heracles, Dionysos, Artemis, Poseidon and Athena, a vast *agora* or public square bordered by porticos, an archaic residential district, a Roman quarter, an odeum and a triumphal arch. A rich collection of sculpture, vases, and bronze and ivory objects is displayed in the museum, open under the plane trees of the old port.

Thasos was in fact a prosperous city in ancient times. The Greeks of Paros, amongst them the poet Archilochus, colonized it in the seventh century. It sold wood, as well as its famous wine. Its strategic position facing a continent which was full of resources but not very secure, its value as a relay station on a great commercial route between Neapolis-Cavalla and Alexandria of Troas, brought it appreciable profits. In the fifth century, it gave Greece the great painter Polygnotus who decorated the 'Lesche' of the Cnidians at Delphi, and the poet, Stesimbrotus. Hippocrates of Cos stayed there for three years and noted in his work clinical observations made on invalids from the island. Thasos suffered many vicissitudes between the Darius' passage in 491 and the Bulgarians' in 1940; but today it experiences only the invasion of tourists.

The name of Samothrace has become famous in the modern period since the French consul Champoiseau discovered the famous, universally known Victory in 1863 and took it back to the Louvre. In ancient times, the renown of the island arose from its sanctuary of the 'Great Gods', the 'Great Mother': the god Kadmilos, the two Cabiri identified by the Greeks with Castor and Pollux, finally Hades and Persephone. These gods of fertility and the hereafter assured a better fate in the other world to those who had themselves initiated into their mysteries. They also protected sailors. There is no better proof of the need for their protection than the coasts of Samothrace, without good anchorage to give shelter from the unceasing gusts of wind which sweep this part of the gulf. Denuded by erosion, the masses of bare granite rise to five thousand feet above the water. From the culminating point, Mount Phengari—or the 'Mountain of the Moon'—there is a marvellous view, from Mount Athos in the west to Mount Ida, which overlooks the plain of Troy. The importance of Samothrace and Thasos is immediately apparent as a stopping point on that great route which took St Paul from Asia to Italy.

It takes five to seven hours by boat, depending on the weather, to go from Alexandropolis to the small Samothracian port of Palaeopolis, near the ruins of the sanctuary where initiation into the mysteries of the 'Great Gods' once took place. Sporadic excavations, carried out by the French (1866), by the Austrians (1863 to 1875), then again by the French (1891 to 1923), were resumed and systematically pursued after 1938 by the University of New York. A museum was built, soon made complete by a modern hotel intended to welcome the numerous tourists attracted by the recent discoveries. The sanctuary comprised a theatre, a large portico, an initiation hall (*Anaktoron*), a monumental rotunda, consecrated by Queen Arsinoe (*Arsinoeion*) for certain sacrifices and sacred banquets, a large temple (*hieron*), various monumental altars, an Ionic propylon joined to a wooden bridge, and finally the great fountain of which the Victory of Samothrace was the chief adornment. Rough natural rocks suggested the outlines of a jetty in the basin, and the Victory, silhouetted against the sky, seemed to be posed on the haughty prow of her boat.

V. A VOYAGE TO THE ISLANDS

OUR adventure begins in Piraeus, amidst all the excitement of a noisy departure. Moored by the stern, the boats from the islands lie alongside each other. The new ones are as white as gulls, the old completely black, their tall yellow funnels striped with white and blue bands like the national flag. The passengers board the boat by a narrow gangway, dragging their cases or wicker baskets, closed with a piece of cloth. All around are the cries of the pedlars and sellers of icons and *loukoums* or crown-shaped rolls—the crisp *coulouria*. The donkey winch fills the hold with its rattling whilst the porters shout out all the well-known names from the Greek calendar: Nico! Costa! Panayote! Sometimes, one of the passengers bursts forth in an irrepressible, volcano-like torrent of imprecation, accompanied by ferocious gestures. Then he suddenly becomes as still as stone, silent, his head sunk in his shoulders, his arms outstretched, his palms turned upwards. His wrath transforms him into a living statue. The full blast of the boat's loudspeaker drowns the surrounding uproar with waves of harmony.

The Greeks have a horror of silence except during the hours of siesta when the slightest noise would be as incongruous as nocturnal disturbance in a western city. Music is as necessary to their happiness as a bracing atmosphere or the company of their fellow men. No car, taxi, or motor coach is without a radio set. The smallest village café has an ancient gramophone with a large trumpet-shaped horn. The joy in living and in being together, the *kefi*, is always expressed in songs, usually sung to guitar accompaniment. These songs are to your ears what the resinous wine is to your throat: you either like it or you do not. Even so, some of the songs, with sharply accentuated rhythms, do attain the level of true poetry. They are popular in the sense that they are sung and danced by the whole Greek people. The musician goes from table to table, striking up his song, and he is as intoxicated as his guests with the joy that he evokes.

The boat leaves. A surprising silence follows the blast from the siren that resounds at the exit from the harbour. The exhausted loudspeaker is hushed. With the muted rhythm of machines in the background, we contemplate the factories of Piraeus, its great concrete silos, the hill of Mounichia covered with yellow houses and, soon, against the bare slopes of Hymettus, Athens comes into sight in the evening mist. Every eye turns to pick out the silhouette of the Parthenon from the compact mass of the city.

Aegina and Hydra are the two islands most easily visited from Athens. One day is enough to see what each is famous for: at Aegina the temple; at

229

Hydra the pirates' harbour, surrounded by the elegant houses of the bourgeoisie who brought about the revolution of 1821.

Aegina is a triangular rock in the Gulf of Athens—'a speck in the eye of Piraeus', according to the Athenians of former days, who envied the prosperity of the island and ended up by chasing away the inhabitants. The people of Aegina were merchants and fine sailors. They owed their wealth to their fleet. They were the first people in Greece to understand the use of money. From the seventh century onwards they began to replace the heavy iron drachmae by pieces of silver bearing the emblem of a tortoise, which were soon circulating in the whole Greek world. They did not disdain the arts. Their bronze founders were famous. At Salamis they won the prize for bravery and proclaimed it to the world by consecrating at Delphi a star of gold borne on a mast. Then the heavy hand of Athens descended on the island and it thenceforth fell into obscurity. But it had nevertheless had time to construct a temple ornamented with sculptured frontons in honour of its goddess Athena-Aphaia.

Supposing this temple did not exist, would people still talk of Aegina? The island is by no means devoid of beauty. By some unknown miracle of tenacity, men have been able to grow pine trees on the mountain, vines, olive trees and pistachio trees (their fruit is wrapped in long twists of cellophane and sold by the pedlars of Athens) in the valleys of this bare rock that has no water supply and no drinking water except from its wells. The harbour has the pleasing cleanliness of all island villages that have been whitewashed over and over again.

But it is the temple that visitors make for. It stands isolated beneath pine trees, dominating the glistening sea that shines emerald six hundred feet below. The first virtue of the temple is that it is still to a large extent upright. Only few antique monuments enjoy this privilege. Outside Athens, one can quickly enumerate the temple of Cape Sunion, that of Apollo at Phigalia-Bassae, three columns at Nemea, seven at Corinth, and some others artificially raised, here and there. The people of Aegina built their temple immediately after Salamis, just before that of Olympia was built, a few years before the Parthenon. In the evolution of the Doric order it is thus possible to follow the rapid progress of Greek genius towards a more and more abstract perfection. In 1812, Prince Ludwig of Bavaria bought the marble sculptures of the frontons. An over-zealous orthopaedist added some arms and legs that were missing. And now the visitor must go to the Munich Museum to see the almond-eyed, strangely smiling Trojans and Greeks confront each other beneath the goddess's partial arbitrament.

An islet that is nothing but a grey rock, flecked here and there with sleek undergrowth, a white port on a blue sea, reflecting dancing caiques, a tangle of masts—Hydra would resemble all the islands of the Cyclades were it not for its grand military and bourgeois air. The circular roadstead is almost enclosed by two promontories bristling with cannons. The ships there seem to be less at rest than caught in ambush. And the houses on the slopes displaying their striking blue-shuttered façades are much more imposing than the village houses of Aegina or Tinos. They do not allow you to forget that they once sheltered the families of notabilities, whose wealth enabled them to equip the revolutionary fleet of 1821. The people of Hydra were fearless sailors. Theirs were the only boats which were not afraid to sail to the Black Sea ports in winter, in search of wheat. As they did not attach overmuch importance to the nuances distinguishing a businessman from a pirate, the revolution soon found well-trained admirals amongst them. There were Tombazis, Tsamados and, above all, the famous Miaoulis, whose moustachioed face is as popular in Greece as that of Kolokotronis. In 1821, Hydra had forty thousand inhabitants but today it has barely three thousand. Peacefully, it dries its sponges in the sun. Nothing disturbs the quiet of its paved streets, as clean as any corridors, or its little square with its fresh and resonant wells—except, that is, for the siren of the Athens boat. At its blast, idlers and strollers gather in the port, curious to see the daily cargo of anxious tourists, with photographs to take and films to make, who will leave as they have come, after a brief sojourn around the iron tables on the café terraces.

There are twenty-four Cyclades. They encircle Delos—hence their name. They are of marble. All that the Peloponnese could offer its artists was an ugly *poros*, a soft stone without dignity. As a result, they had recourse to metal and became famous bronze workers. The artists of the Cyclades worked in marble. From the prehistoric epoch onwards, with no instrument but a polishing tool, they have patiently carved stylized statuettes of goddesses, their arms folded on their breasts, out of this fine material—'the guardian of the pure contour'. The same men were also responsible for what is an astonishing *tour de force* when one thinks of their lack of technical equipment—the inspired harpist in the National Museum, found on the island of Amorgos. A man of Naxos was the first to conceive the idea of carving tiles in marble; and during the archaic epoch the graceful troop of broad-shouldered athletic *couroi* was hewn from the compact Parian marble or the Naxian marble with its heavy grain. The same period also saw the first smile on the countenance of Greek art—with the full figures of the *cores* beneath the complexity of their finery.

The Cyclades have no wealth other than their stones. The rocks are swept almost the whole year round by a violent north wind, known as the *Vorias*— until summer comes when it changes its name to *Meltem*. As a result, vegetation is sparse. Amongst the aloes, the cacti and the fig trees, a few vines and thin blades of corn struggle on the few acres of fertile soil, pinned to the slopes by terraced walls of dry stones. Here and there the aridity is alleviated inland from the coasts, and the more sheltered valleys are covered with olive trees, forests of ilex and almond trees. But water is always in short supply.

Santorin has nothing but rain to rely on to quench its thirst. Drinking water has often to be brought to the island by boat. Delos drinks from the reservoirs found in its ancient houses.

The beauty of the Cyclades arises from their mineral-laden soil, its iridescent shades changing as the day advances, from a more intense luminosity than is found elsewhere, and from the painted caiques in the white roadsteads, which recall all the poetry of a perpetual Odyssey.

The Cyclades belonged to Venice after the Fourth Crusade. Venice left them with strong castles, the evil memory of its mercantile spirit and a population mostly converted to Catholicism. Tinos, the most Catholic of all, is also, paradoxically, the centre of the greatest Greek Orthodox pilgrimage in honour of the Virgin. In 1822 a miraculous icon was discovered. Since then, the church of Our Lady of Good Tidings welcomes beneath its white porticos, every March 25 and August 15, crowds of sick and infirm who have come from all over Greece to pray for recovery.

It was at Tinos that we first took part in the ceremony of a Greek Orthodox Easter. In Western Europe, the Christian festival *par excellence* is Christmas, celebrated by believers and unbelievers in a common joy. For the Greeks there is no greater festival than Easter. Greek Orthodoxy always sees God in His most transcendent aspects. It celebrates less the birth which made Him man than the resurrection which proclaims His divinity. During the centuries of servitude, Easter seemed a symbol of confidence and hope: 'Christ is risen, my brothers,' says a character of the novelist Kazantzakis, 'Greece will also rise.'

The boat which took us to Mykonos cast anchor in the harbour of Tinos shortly before midnight in order to allow the passengers to take part in the ceremony. Just as we disembarked, a procession set out towards a chapel perched on the heights. We bought a candle tied with a blue ribbon and followed the black-bearded priests in their finery, chanting psalms amidst the lantern-carriers. In the narrow streets, each marble paving-stone had been encircled with whitewash. The freshly painted houses were radiantly white. The chapel, isolated beside an olive tree, soon came in sight, looking as tiny and as white as the houses. It overlooked the roadsteads, only visible in the darkness because of a green light. The church door was closed. We sang psalms. Suddenly it was midnight. The priest struck three tremendous blows on the door. The door opened. 'Christ is risen.' The noise was enormous, repeated by everyone present, embracing and wishing each other many more happy years. Then the illuminated town burst forth from its darkness. The sea was covered with boats outlined by electric lights. Bells rang out. Rockets and crackers went off. The noise of sirens and rifle shots created the atmosphere of noisy devotion and popular rejoicing which elsewhere acclaims the birth of a prince or a victorious armistice. Then each one brought the Paschal candle home, shielding its flickering flame with his hands. It was a pledge of happiness for the year. Everyone ended a strict forty days' fast by eating until dawn lamb roasted on a spit, and the Easter cake, the *tsoureki* stuck with red eggs.

Mykonos is the most Cycladian of the Cyclades and an obligatory stopping place before reaching Delos. However accustomed he is to the islands of the Aegean, Mykonos always surprises the visitor when its flat-roofed houses come into sight at the back of the harbour, like a vision of Africa. Only the windmills have thatched roofs and only the churches have red domes. There are so many tiny chapels on the slopes that it is difficult to distinguish them. They were consecrated by the people of Mykonos to their patron saints in the same way as, earlier, a treasury was built to the gods of Delphi and Olympia.

It is a real pleasure to climb the streets paved with marble, with a gutter running down the middle, that re-echo to the slightest step in the silence of the siesta. It is a pleasure to stand in the shadow of an arcade. A half-open door reveals a courtyard of freshly washed pebbles, an end of a climbing vine, a clump of laurel. A woman at a casement window is weaving at her handloom the local cloth—red, black or blue, striped with gold bands. The house is as white inside as out. It has been whitewashed so often that the corners are rounded with the thickness of all the whitewash that has been applied. On the ground floor there are workshops, stables and storerooms. The principal room is almost always one floor up, joined to the street by an outside staircase. The icons are heaped on a shelf in a corner, next to the copper censer and the night-light used each evening. The bed is always makeshift, easily drawn out on to the terrace and hidden beneath vividly coloured blankets.

At Mykonos we leave the steamboats of the regular shipping lines and embark for Delos. From his comfortable petrol-driven boat, the tourist may perhaps see a caique with a high prow and trumpet-shaped sides being loaded with cows and goats sent by the people of Mykonos for summer pasturage on Delos or Rhenea. Confusion and excitement always precede the caique's departure. There is no disembarkation problem. Goats, lambs and cows are tipped ashore by vigorous blows and shoulder thrusts. They land miraculously on all fours, already on their way to the salty meadows.

Delos is three miles long and almost one mile wide at its maximum. It has very little water. Nothing predestined Delos to be anything but a deserted islet, at most a grazing ground for cattle during the summer—to be precise, what it was from the time of the ruin of the sanctuary of Apollo until the excavations of the French School of Athens brought it once more to attention at the end of the last century. Its very insignificance, because it disarmed jealousy, marked it out as a communal sanctuary for all the inhabitants of the Aegean.

But the ancient peoples thought that only a decree of the divine will could explain the fame of such a bare rock. Leto, they said, had to wander from island to island in search of shelter to give birth to the son she had conceived by Zeus. Every island, fearing retaliation from Hera, the legitimate wife of Zeus, rejected her. Delos, because it had nothing to lose, welcomed her. She gave birth to Apollo in the shade of a palm tree which was then, as now, the only tree on the island. She paid her debt of gratitude to Delos by making the island one of the great pan-Hellenic sanctuaries of the classical world. Apollo was worshipped there but also his sister Artemis and his mother Leto, whose temple was joined to the port of Skardana by a Sacred Way lined with great lions in marble from Naxos, as slim as greyhounds. During the centuries, as Delos became the *entrepôt* for the whole Mediterranean, the merchants of Egypt and Syria added their own divinities to Greek worship. Multiple chapels to the Syrian goddess, and Egyptian sanctuaries with long rows of sphinxes were erected on Mount Cynthos. In the theatre and port districts traders built houses richly decorated with paintings and mosaics.

Thus Delos can offer a group of ruins unique in Greece for extent and variety. Neither Olympia nor Delphi gives the same impression of immensity. All those bare walls, that white marble stretching out of sight along the burnt soil, shine in the sunlight like bones on the desert. One is reminded of some valley of Jehoshaphat. And when night falls on the ruins of the dead city, the watcher has a strange feeling of loneliness—a sort of *Angst* barely relieved by the marvellous sight of the sun setting over the Cyclades.

At Delos, as at Delphi and Olympia, the great men of the day wanted to use the religious prestige of the sanctuary to serve their politics. The sanctuaries went at least as far back as the Mycenean epoch, as is proved by beautiful ivories found beneath the temple of Artemis. The people of Naxos in the seventh century BC covered the island with their offerings—an extremely archaic-type building, a portico, and various statues, one of which is a colossal marble Apollo. All that remains are *membra disjecta*—a decapitated torso, a fragment of thigh, one hand at Delos, a foot in London; and a sketch by a seventeenth-century traveller to the deserted island who saw the enormous head of the god, still in place on his shoulders, rearing up from the heap of marbles which had not yet been consumed by the lime kilns. The whiteness of the Cyclades over the centuries unfortunately consisted of the marbles of Delos reduced to lime.

Domination by Athens was the most long-lasting and also the most harsh. It could draw its authority from old legends: Apollo had rid the island of the wild goats that infested it and built an altar with their horns—the Keraton. When the Athenian prince, Theseus, and his companions landed on the island on their return from Crete, they performed a dance with complicated meanderings around the altar, reproducing the turnings in the Labyrinth where the Minotaur had been vanquished. And every four years the Athenians danced the same roundelay for the great festival of Delia.

The force of Athenian imperialism was really felt after the Persian wars.

In order to prevent the return of the Persians, it united the islands of the Aegean in a confederation with its capital at Delos. The federal treasury, fed by the contributions of the allies of Athens, was placed under the protection of Apollo. But in 454, on the pretext of ensuring greater safety, Athens moved it to her own soil. A large part of the funds were allocated to embellishing the Acropolis. To the protesting allies, Pericles replied: 'What are you complaining about? You pay a fee to be protected from the Persians. Does the Athenian fleet not see that your coasts are respected? Athens fulfils her obligations towards you. It matters little to you the uses to which she puts the sums you pay out.'

When Athens fell victim to attacks from Sparta in 404, Delos regained its autonomy for a time. But it only became truly independent again at the end of the fourth century BC. The island then knew a prosperity which reached its height in the second century when the Romans transformed it into a free port. But the people of Delos were no longer there to enjoy it. For reasons of political opportunism, Rome, flying in the face of all justice, gave the island to the Athenians, who expelled all the native population. Delos then became a city of traders and bankers, grouped in associations under the protection of a god. Each group had its place of assembly near the great depôts and warehouses where vessels from all over the Mediterranean—Syria, Egypt, Italy—were moored in the sheltered harbour. Perhaps it was a boat from Delos that was sunk with its cargo of amphorae off the coast of Provence and on which the name of a rich Delian has apparently been identified.

The prosperity of Delos suddenly collapsed. The admirals of Mithridates massacred the twenty-five thousand Romans living in the town. The pirate Athenodorus ravaged the sanctuary and carried what remained of the population into slavery. Insecurity in the Aegean led to the abandonment of the island—still covered with statues and monuments. Athens tried to sell it but found no buyers. A few Christian communities were not enough to bring life back to Delos and it soon became nothing but a marble quarry consumed day and night by lime kilns, in the heart of the Cyclades.

At first it is somewhat difficult to find one's way about the sanctuary of Apollo. As at Olympia the monuments lie stretched out in confusion on the ground. Pausanias unfortunately left no description of Delos and we would be in some difficulty if we did not possess the accounts of the guardians of the sanctuary engraved on marble. These were four *hierops* who administered and supervised the upkeep of the edifices. As these inscriptions list the monuments in a certain order, it has been possible, too, to identify others hitherto unknown by using certain known points of reference. Thus the three temples of Apollo have been identified, as well as the sanctuary of Artemis, the temple of Leto, that of the twelve gods and many other constructions. The great Hellenistic porticos of Antigonus and of Philip V, the 'club' of Beirut merchants protected by Poseidon, the *agora* of the Italian merchants grouped beneath the aegis of

Hermes and the 'sanctuary of the bulls' which sheltered a man-of-war probably offered to the god by Demetrius Poliorcetes—all these, with their large-scale architecture, surrounded the monuments of the Hellenic sanctuary in much the same way as the double colonnade of the high Stoa of Attalos crushed the older edifices of the *agora* of Athens.

The private houses of Delos appeal to the imagination even more than the temples, being perhaps more evocative of human presence, with terra-cotta stoves, marble tables and with the lips of the wells furrowed with smooth channels by the cords' rubbing. Their walls of greenish gneiss still stand at a good height along the narrow, climbing roads, similar to those at Mykonos. Windows on the outside are rare; the whole house draws its daylight from the square courtyard edged by a marble peristyle, where the ground generally covers a reservoir. Many of these reservoirs are still intact, and the fishermen of the Cyclades who put in at Delos draw their fresh water in the 'House of Cleopatra' across the lips of ancient wells. Superb mosaics decorate the floor of the courtyard and the state-rooms. Only rare fragments remain of the paintings and the stucco which once covered their walls with a richness comparable to that of the houses of Pompeii; but no protecting lava came to give them shelter.

Although the mountain of Cynthos is only three hundred and fifty feet high, its steep rocks exposed to the Meltem seem to raise you right up in the air, so that its actual height is scarcely credible. You overlook the whole of Delos, the stadium, the palaestras, the vast hollow of the theatre, the labyrinth of streets, the outline of the sanctuary (seen much more clearly from a bird's-eye view), the shops along the port, the Bay of Phourni, the sanctuary of Asclepios, and the rest of the island, partitioned by dry stone walls, which delimit the properties of the Mykoniates. Granite columns rise half-way above the ground in fields of oats, giving birth to conjectures about buried houses and the mosaics and statues they may still conceal. And all around the horizon are the petrified silhouettes of the Cyclades, blue in the morning, violet in the evening; in the north, Mykonos, Tinos and Syros; Seriphos in the west; in the south, Siphnos, rich for a time from its gold mines, Paros and its marble, and the large island of Naxos where Theseus abandoned Ariadne. The ungrateful conqueror pretended to attribute his victory not to the princess's thread but rather to the protection of Apollo and, deaf to the pleas of his deserted betrothed, came and danced round the altar of the horns with the seven young men and the seven maidens whom he had saved from the appetite of the Minotaur.

Santorin (called Thera by the Greeks and Santa Irini by the Venetians) was first named Strongyle from the Greek *strongylos* which means 'round', because it was as round as a pebble. Then, a thousand years before Christ, the whole centre of the island caved in and what had once been the crater of a marble volcano became a marine basin, where islands appeared and disappeared, at the mercy of eruptions and earth tremors. The limestone islets which emerge from the bay are no more than four centuries old. The great eruption of 1925 once again modified the relief. A crater smokes at the summit. Not greatly perturbed by this formidable proximity, the inhabitants of Santorin grow grapes in terraces on the slopes facing the outward side of the island, from which they make a heady wine. Together with *pozzolana* it is their sole wealth. The ambitious have to seek their fortune elsewhere or turn to the sea. Santorin is the home of the great ship-owners.

The Greek countryside owes its beauty to the secret harmony of its colours and its lines, rarely to the grandeur of its proportions or to those natural curiosities which are attractive because they are astounding, and which one tires of when they lose the attraction of novelty. There are scarcely any exceptions to this, apart from the Meteors and Santorin. The fractured edge of Santorin, a wall a thousand feet high, reddened, blackened, cut with white streaks of *pozzolana*—that cargo boats load directly from the mountain into their holds as the slope is so steep—gives the impression of disaster and seems to bring to our attention, as if they had happened yesterday, all the geological catastrophes which engulfed a continent beneath the waves of the Aegean and left nothing but the Cyclades. The roadstead is so deep that boats cannot anchor there. You generally land below Phira where the houses are a white streak separating cliff from sky. Small asses carry you along dizzy hairpin bends up to the village where the view is magnificent. But perhaps the village of Oia at the northern point of the island, where one scarcely halts, is still more picturesque than Phira. Houses there are built by pouring *pozzolana* on to large blocks of earth which form a sort of negative of the building; when the *pozzolana* has hardened, the earth which supported it is removed; there remains a sort of hollow shell, all in one piece, which no earth tremor in the world can possibly shake.

*
* *

Crete is admirably situated, not far from the Cypriot copper mines, at the maritime cross-roads of three continents. She is joined to the Peloponnese by Cythera and Anticythera, prolonged towards the Asiatic coast by Carpathos and Rhodes, bathed in the north by the Aegean scattered with islands, a homely sea where there is always some land in sight, and in the south by the Sea of Libya, a deserted expanse swept by winds which, according to the season, blow ships from Crete to Egypt and from Egypt to Crete. Her position was the foundation of the commercial prosperity which for a thousand years nourished the most ancient civilization worthy of the name ever to have appeared on European soil. Afterwards, for the same reasons, the isle was coveted by every people that wanted to dominate the Aegean Sea: the Byzantines, the Arabs, the Venetians, the Turks, and finally the Germans who parachuted down on to its soil in 1940. It has always played a special part in Greek history. The hazards of European diplomacy only restored it to the motherland in 1913, although of all Greeks the Cretans gave most trouble to the successive occupants of their land. Their accent and their physical type in themselves distinguish them from other Greeks. They are generally tall, slim, tanned, with black eyes and a virile step. They wear black kerchiefs with short fringes on their heads, and above leather boots the baggy bottoms of their black trousers serve as shopping baskets. Of a liberal tradition, they worship the memory of E. Venizelos, of whom plaster busts wearing caps of blue felt are sold.

The arrival at Crete by sea is a really beautiful sight. It must be seen at the break of day when the sun skims this long, high mountainous barrier rising sheer out of the waves. Hollowed with blue shadows, the groups of mountains stand out in successive levels, growing paler and paler. If a patch of snow, lingering into the springtime, did not mark the summit of Mount Ida at an altitude of just over eight thousand feet, it too would be indistinct in the luminous mist of distance. The traveller who arrives at the port of Heraklion, at the very foot of Mount Ida, glimpses in the east the strange silhouetted profile of Mount Jouktas, like a bearded mask abandoned by a gigantic tragedian. This is how Crete appeared to the Athenian, Theseus, when he landed at the port of Knossos to confront the Minotaur and deliver his native land from its odious burden.

Heraklion has not the picturesque charm of the Canaea. On entering the port one notices first a bastion emblazoned with the lion of St Mark, then, in large metallic letters on the roof of a hotel, the name of King Minos. This serves as an announcement of the essential items of interest at Crete: its Venetian monuments and its Minoan antiquities. But the works of Morosini are far surpassed by those of Minos and his contemporaries.

This Minoan civilization seems to have dawned about 3400 BC. It developed around 2400, when the Egyptians were constructing their pyramids, reached its culminating point around 1700 and collapsed abruptly in about 1400, approximately two centuries before the Trojan War. Between the terminal dates twenty centuries flowed silently by, leaving no trace; and they were lost without bequeathing the mention of a single historical event, the name of a single artist—except the legendary Daedalus—or of a single king—except the legendary Minos. These twenty centuries, however, are known to have seen the flowering of a great maritime empire, together with one of the most exquisite expressions of Mediterranean art.

Until the beginning of the twentieth century, the name of Crete meant the same to scholars as it had always done: a land of legend, haunted by the fabulous shades of Minos, Pasiphaë, Phaedra and Ariadne. Questioned as to the history of the island, a Greek of antiquity would undoubtedly have begun with the fable of the little Zeus threatened by the appetite of his father, Cronos. But Rhea, his mother, offered Cronos a stone wrapped in swaddling clothes in place of the child, whom she hid in Crete, in a grotto of Mount Ida. The bees and the nymphs fed him with honey, the goat Amalthaea with milk; while the Couretes, the spirits of the mountains, in order to soothe or cover the wailing of the newborn child, danced and clashed their shields of bronze—the Cretans were among the first to learn how to smelt and work metal.

Promoted to leader of the gods in place of Cronos, Zeus chose the island which had sheltered him in childhood to shelter his loves. The daughter of the King of the Phoenicians was playing on the shore at Sidon one day; she was of startling beauty, and was known as Europa. Aflame with love, Zeus changed himself into a white bull with horns like the crescent moon; he slept at the feet of the girl, who at first was afraid, but soon caressed the animal and sat on its back. Then he carried her across the waves to Crete and married her near a spring at Gortyne, in a grove where the plane trees thenceforth had the privilege of never losing their leaves. Thus were conceived the three brothers, Minos, Rhadamanthus and Sarpedon.

When they were old enough to be kings, Minos claimed the title for himself alone: the gods, he said, could refuse him nothing. As proof of this, Poseidon at his request made a bull rise from the sea. This bull was so beautiful that when Minos became king he neglected to sacrifice it as he had promised—an omission which the god did not hesitate to avenge. After pursuing numerous nymphs and also, it is said, a few young men, during a tumultuous adolescence, Minos married Pasiphaë, the daughter of the Sun, by whom he had two daughters, Ariadne and Phaedra. At her first sight of the bull of Poseidon, the queen was seized by a strange passion: the Minotaur was born as a result of it, a monster with the body of a man and the head of a bull.

At this time, an Athenian artist named Daedalus lived at the court at Knossos; he ministered to the queen's deviant purposes by constructing a heifer of wood for her to hide in. He was ordered to build a princely residence where the unfortunate Minotaur should pass his life, far from the regard of the curious and without power ever to leave it. This was the Labyrinth. Since it was also necessary to provide some distraction for it, Minos, who held the Athenians responsible for the accidental death of his son Androgeos, imposed on them, by way of reparation, payment of an annual tribute of seven young men and seven young women, dedicated to the appetite of the monster.

At this point, Theseus, son of Aegeus, a young Athenian prince, intervened. He volunteered to make the journey to Crete. His youth, his noble bearing made the most lively impression on the Princess Ariadne the moment he arrived at Knossos. She wanted him to escape from the Labyrinth and asked advice from Daedalus. Athenian solidarity here came into play, and Daedalus worked out a plan using the ball of thread. Theseus entered the Labyrinth, killed the Minotaur and found his way out thanks to the ball of thread. He left Crete with his companions, carrying off Ariadne—but later marrying Phaedra. However, as he approached Athens, he forgot to change his black sail for the white one which was to have announced his victory. The aged Aegeus was watching for his son's return from the heights of the Acropolis. Seeing the sail plunged in mourning, he was mad with grief, and threw himself into the shimmering sea—about five miles away!—which since then has borne his name. Theseus became king. Evil tongues claimed that the omission to change the sail was not just the result of thoughtlessness. But no rapid rise can ever take place without immediately inspiring the slander of the envious. . . .

Meanwhile, Minos began to think that Daedalus' activities were somewhat indiscreet: first the wooden heifer, now the ball of thread. . . . The artist was interned in the now vacant Labyrinth, in company with Icarus, his son by a servant from the palace. But Daedalus was a universal genius. As a sculptor, he had replaced the ancient stiff-legged statues by statues shown in motion. As an engineer, Crete owed to him a bronze robot-sentinel which watched over the safety of its shores. In order to escape the Labyrinth and also the watchfulness of the automatic sentinel, Daedalus chose to travel by air. The imprudent Icarus rose to too high an altitude, and the wax which held the feathers of his wings melted so that he was precipitated into the waves. As for Daedalus, he reached Sicily without mishap. Minos pursued him right to the residence of King Cocalos. Evil befell him there: Daedalus secretly modified the plumbing of his bathroom and King Minos perished, boiled alive in his bath. Then, attended by Aeacus and Rhadamanthus, 'Minos judged in Hades all the pale humans'.

This gilded—though somewhat scandalous—legend took the place of any history of ancient Crete right up to the beginning of the twentieth century. Excavations on the site of the palace of Knossos, conducted from 1900 to 1905 by Sir Arthur Evans, inaugurated a new epoch. Archaeology did not destroy the legends. It illustrated them most strikingly, and the tangle of the Labyrinth can be seen today in the winding palaces at Knossos, Mallia and Phaestos. We can contemplate on the walls of the Museum of Heraklion the powerful beauty of the bull of Poseidon, charging acrobats who dodge it with airy leaps.

When he undertook excavations at Knossos, Evans did not have at his disposal any framework of chronological reference, because the historic past of 'Minoan' Crete was—and remains—for the most part a blank. The English scholar therefore paid the greatest attention to the succession of archaeological layers which had been superimposed in the course of centuries to a depth of over thirty feet. Some of these layers could fortunately be dated by a few Egyptian objects which they contained. On the evidence of these rare fixed points, and by taking into account the sequence of the layers and their thickness,

Evans laid the basis of a chronology, the broad lines of which are still valid today: after a neolithic period of at least ten thousand years, there began around 3400, and lasted for two millenia, the 'Minoan' civilization. This is conventionally divided into three broad periods, called Ancient Minoan, Middle Minoan and Recent Minoan, which in turn are each subdivided into three periods. Within this broad framework archaeologists try to classify their discoveries, in an attempt to snatch a fragment of history out of obscurity.

Of the Cretans themselves, anthropology can deduce that they were small, but their figures were so well proportioned that, seen in action on their frescoes, they seem tall, slender and muscular. The men are shown bronzed by the sun, clad in clinging slips which expose their vigorous athletic silhouettes; the women white as lilies, their flesh full and firm in their fluffy floating dresses. Their dwellings were middle-class houses with one or two floors, covered with terraces, which the faience of Knossos has depicted for us. There were also princely palaces which we know well from the English excavations at Knossos, the Italian excavations at Phaestos and the French excavations at Mallia. They had state-rooms of monumental proportions, private apartments which softened lighting, from pools of light, bathed with freshness and intimacy, dark store-rooms where—a striking picture of opulence—oil and grain in large jars as high as a man were lined up. These the potter had encircled with a cable design. All this surrounded a vast central courtyard in a disorder which was more apparent than real. This architecture presupposed the existence of a society with a feudal structure or of a powerful monarchy. One of these kings might have been Minos, unless all the kings of Crete bore the title of Minos. It seems that the kings were also the high priests. Crete, which built such beautiful palaces for men, did not erect a temple for its gods. It worshipped them either in the small chapels of the palace, or more often in the grottoes in the sides of the mountains and on the peaks. It seems that the principal divinity was a great goddess of fertility, accompanied by a male god who was subordinate to her. It seems also that the sacred trees, the bull—victim or hypostasis of the god— and the double axe played a considerable part in the rites of this religion. But the uncertainty surrounding it all is immense. The frescoes and the engraved stones unfold a series of stories without words which we are reduced to interpreting by using more or less science, audacity and ingenuity but, generally, abundant comment. When history is silent, the historian has a lot to say.

One is on more solid ground in discussing Cretan art. The results of half a century of excavation assembled in the museum at Heraklion illustrate the richness and the variety of the Cretans' genius. In this stupendous art, there is little or none at all of the great sculpture that the Greeks brought to perfection. Exceptionally gifted, the Cretan artist in gold excelled in bending the golden guard of a sword into the shape of an acrobat; he reproduced a hunt along the length of a spear; he joined two fragile bees face to face in a delicate pendant. As a ceramist, susceptible to the charm of the nature surrounding him, he decorated his vases with large flowers with bending stalks, with marine animals, with octopi unfolding their sucker-spotted tentacles in supple arabesques. He translated on to his frescoes the feline walk of a watchful cat, the joyful bounding of dolphins, the petulant glance of a young woman with an upturned nose, as well as the power of a charging bull. The true symbol of this diverse talent, which passed easily from force to grace, seems to us to be the fresco at Knossos which shows acrobats leaping airily as they frolic with a massive bull with long horns.

Poetic and spiritual, loving the comfort and charm of life, refined without affectation, this civilization disappeared irrevocably at the end of the fifteenth century BC. Invasion? Earth tremor? It has been discussed to little purpose. Something had gone which the world was not to see again.

In the neighbourhood of Heraklion, the countryside is undulating, with soft hills covered with olive trees and vines. The Cretans make their grapes into a light wine and a highly scented white brandy, the *tsikoudia*. In this pleasant setting, Knossos, sheltered by pine trees, preserves the ruins of its fabulous palace. The first impression may be deceptive for, seen from afar, there is nothing to distinguish the bare walls and apartments cut in two from modern bombed buildings. Once in the palace, the size of its conception is astounding. The succession of great state-rooms, which discreet restorations help one to reconstruct in the imagination, evokes a royal grandeur. The Cretan architects conceived buildings not from the exterior but from the interior. There is no façade in the architectural sense of the term: the palace is shaped round the central courtyard from which it draws its daylight and which joins the diverse 'islands' of habitations.

At first there seems to be no plan behind this jumble of rooms, stairways, pools of light, this labyrinth of winding corridors. But in reality, logical thought lay behind the apparent chaos. The state-rooms, administrative premises, warehouses and storerooms, where the king accumulated the products of his domains, are grouped to the west of the courtyard. The private living quarters form a compact block opposite the latter on the east. The reception rooms on the west are situated on the first floor, *piano nobile*. The plan can be read on the reconstructed platform which covers and protects the remains of the ground floor. These vast rooms are reached either directly from the courtyard by a central stairway, or by a wide flight of steps contained between two propylons. One of them has been partially reconstructed with its famous fresco of vase-carriers. The proportions are ample, the design airy. The rooms open on to the exterior by windows with multiple bays; on to the courtyard by a long colonnaded gallery. The 'throne room' with benches and dolphins painted on a fresco is on the ground floor. A long corridor separates this group of rooms from the warehouses, oblong storerooms arranged in parallel lines like the teeth of a comb.

The rooms in the private living quarters again attain noble proportions. But the architect has treated them in a totally different spirit. They are as though folded back on themselves, at least in the part which remains. The hall of the double axes, the stairway which leads to it, the charming 'megaron of the queen' with its fresco of dolphins, are lit by narrow pools of light, with no outlook on to the exterior. However, the inhabitants were not entirely shut up. Frescoes show the beautiful ladies of the palace at their window on the first floor engaged in watching some spectacle taking place in the courtyard—or perhaps in the 'theatrical enclosure', a quadrangular esplanade located at the north-west entrance, bordered on two sides by tiers at right angles. Perhaps this is the dancing place which Homer still remembered. The Iliad tells of the marvellous shield of Achilles which showed 'a dancing floor like the one that Daedalus designed in the spacious town of Knossos for Ariadne of the lovely locks'.

Frescoes previously covered the indifferent masonry, now so unflattering to the appearance of these ruins. Some have been preserved and can be found at the Museum of Heraklion. Copies, installed in their place, help the imagination to represent the strange atmosphere created by their warm colours in the subdued light of the corridors, by an architecture which made no attempt to satisfy the intelligence, but in the sudden brightness of a well of light or in the turn of a corridor was designed to store up constant surprises for the feelings.

Compared with that at Knossos, the palace at Mallia presents a provincial aspect. Of the same glorious red as the earth in which it has been buried for more than three thousand years, the palace is of modest dimensions yet none the less original in its architecture, with its porticos and, overlooking the courtyard, the monumental façade of its official apartments. At Knossos, at Phaestos, it is easy to lose one's way in an inextricable maze of buildings. At Mallia, because of the reduced scale of the building, the arrangement of a Cretan palace can be more conveniently seen in its entirety. Here, as elsewhere, it developed around a rectangular courtyard, the centre occupied by a curious installation pertaining to worship—an altar or a pit for libations—which emphasizes its religious character. Such courtyards were not, in fact, used only for social gatherings, but were also the background to religious ceremonies. Some archaeologists even think that the sacred 'bull races', shown on frescoes, actually took place in the courtyards of the palaces.

The courtyard of Mallia was dignified by a portico, with alternating columns and pillars, on the two sides which faced the entrance and the royal apartments respectively. This architectural decoration concealed storerooms—which have been partly reconstructed—provided with an ingenious system of drains for the recovery of spilt oil. The state-rooms, to which a flight of steps gave access, opened on to the courtyard through a double bay with a central column. The frescoes help us to imagine the women of high birth in full regalia following from this loggia the spectacle presented in the courtyard. A circular marble table for offerings, a *kernos*, sealed into the paving at the entrance to a small chapel, gathered together in numerous small cups the first-fruits of harvests which the owners of the palace wished to place beneath the protection of the divinity. They made good use of their resources; and the ceremonial arms which have been found in the palace, swords with golden hilts, and bronze hatchets, are evidence of princely taste. Around the ruined palace in the plain, between the mountain and the sea, windmills with white sails unceasingly pump water to the orange and lemon orchards.

Of the three palaces, Phaestos is the most refined. Its external appearance corresponds most to the idea of Cretan art that is formed after a visit to the museum at Heraklion. The beautiful structure of its walls is more pleasing than the less spectacular masonry of Mallia and Knossos. Above all, Phaestos possesses its admirable background. Perched on a raised mound, it overlooks the plain of Mesara, a vast fertile corridor which crosses Crete from north to south between the masses of Mount Ida and Mount Dicte. In the distance, as far as the empty horizon, shines the Sea of Libya. The entrance to the palace was on the west. An imposing stairway, bordered by a paved esplanade over one hundred feet wide, led to a monumental porch divided into two bays by an axial column. Various corridors led to the principal courtyard which was of truly royal proportions (seventy-five by one hundred and seventy feet) and paved in stone. It was previously bordered on the east and west by porticos. To the north, two engaged columns framed the door of a long corridor flanked with two recesses. Around this architectural kernel, the various living quarters were arranged. The dwelling rooms of the royal family were probably on the north with its marvellous view of Mount Ida. The most profane tourist, even in the course of the most rapid visit, takes away a striking impression of a princely residence that has been styled 'the most beautiful architectural success of the bronze age in the Near East'.

In the evening there is a luminous enchantment when the sun holds sway: the dark-blue silhouette of Ida is outlined against the light of a red and green sky; Dicte is nothing but a block of clear amethyst shaded with violet in the hollow of the valleys, while the plain progressively darkens, overcome by the shadow of Ida, returning the palace to its solitude and its ghosts.

VI. RHODES

R HODES is like a large ship anchored very near to the Asiatic coast. Its figure-head is the town of Rhodes which has the same name as the whole island. Fifty miles long and covering an area of eight hundred and fifteen square miles, it is the most important of the Twelve Islands (or Dodecanese), of which it constitutes the natural capital. The three summits of the mountainous masses of St Elias, Atramytis and Atabyros (which reaches its highest point at four thousand feet) rise in the heart of undulating hills, where the torrents brutally cut great white trails in winter. A plain edged by beaches follows the line of the coast, which here is not particularly indented, and ports are rare. Those at Lindos and Rhodes are excellent and have made the fortunes of the two towns.

The gentle, relatively humid climate favours vegetation, surprisingly exuberant to the visitor from Attica or the Cyclades. Pines suitable for naval construction, cypresses sought by cabinet-makers and olive and fig trees, large planes around fountains, terebinths, carob trees, palm trees and banana trees with their large hanging leaves are more than an adornment—they are a source of wealth. To delight the eye there is also the striking effect of broom and mimosa in winter, the warm colours of the bougainvillaeas and the paler shades of the oleanders in summer. 'A cluster of greenery in the bosom of the waves', 'a flower broken off from the bank, a rose of the Archipelago, European and Asiatic at the same time'—the succession of travellers and conquerors have been as much aware of the attractions of the island as of her interesting position as a staging point between Asia Minor and the Aegean world.

Rhodes entered Greek history when bands of Dorian adventurers, coming from Argos and Lacedaemon on the advice of the Oracle of Delphi, founded the three cities of Ialysos, Camiros and Lindos. The towns rapidly grew prosperous and in their turn spread through the whole Mediterranean basin. They participated in the foundation of Parthenopus (which became Naples), and of Gela (where Agrigentum was built). Well before the arrival of the Phocaeans at Marseilles, the Rhodians landed on the coasts of France and gave the name of Rhodanoussia to the city which could have been the ancestor of Arles. This expansion led to intense commercial activity. The ships the Rhodians constructed from wood from their forests carried to countries abroad oil, wine, figs, jewellery and arms from Ialysos, as well as beautiful clay vases, dishes, cups and pitchers, finely decorated with animals—spotted deer and does, lions, bulls and fabulous griffins, or quite simply with a flock of geese waddling along. The museum at Rhodes also preserves monumental red-clay jars with designs engraved on them. Sometimes more than six feet high, their large size made them unsuitable for export. They were used at Rhodes to keep stocks of oil or wheat, and at times to serve as the final resting place for their owner!

At the end of the fifth century BC, the three Rhodian cities founded a city in common at the northern point of the island, entrusting the great town planner Hippodamos of Miletus with its construction. Thus Rhodes was born. It was one of the most beautiful as well as one of the best fortified cities of antiquity. Although a careful policy attempted to preserve its prosperity amidst the quarrels of Greece, the city became involved in the rivalries dividing Alexander's successors. Rhodes had concluded an alliance with the Ptolemies of Egypt. To punish her for this, Antigonus of Syria, a rival of the Ptolemies, sent his son Demetrius to attack the celebrated walls of the city in the year 305. One of the seven wonders of the world, the Colossus of Rhodes, was born as a result of this unsuccessful siege.

Demetrius, then quite a young man, was already marked out for attention by his contemporaries because of his exceptional talents as an engineer in the most diverse fields. He had designed enormous warships which were so perfectly balanced that, according to Plutarch, they could be manœuvred like simple boats. Taking up a project already formed by the tyrant of Corinth, Periander, he studied how to cut the Isthmus of Corinth. But he owed his nickname of Poliorcetes—the besieger—to his speciality: the siege of cities. Before Rhodes, he employed all his genius. Long afterwards, admiration was still evoked by memory of the armoured ships which led the attack from the sea; while on land, battering rams and improved catapults (from which enormous stone balls have been found) hammered unceasingly on the ramparts. But the most amazing machine was the great helepole, a wooden tower mounted on wheels, one hundred and thirty feet high, whence the besiegers were able to overlook the besieged. It was a masterpiece of carpentry but the Rhodians succeeded in driving away this danger, causing it to run aground in an artificial swamp. The obstinacy of the defenders defeated the genius of Demetrius who had to retire, abandoning all his siege equipment to the Rhodians. They sold it and consecrated the proceeds to the erection of a gigantic bronze statue, representing the Sun, the protecting god of the island, which recalled this memorable victory at the entrance to the port on the present site of St Nicholas's Tower. This was the famous Colossus of Rhodes. It soon became so famous that the old Dorian word *colossos*, which originally designated all standing statues, no matter what their size, has since taken on the meaning it has today. The ancient peoples admired the skill shown in casting a statue a hundred feet high even more than its artistic value. Chares of Lindos worked twelve years on end casting the bronze in an earthen mould. This was progressively raised higher, by horizontal sections, to the degree that the Colossus rose in the sky, within a gigantic scaffolding, doubtless made from materials from the wood of the great helepole. When the work was finished, sailors approaching the port could see, to quote an epigram, a second sun shining as high in the sky over Rhodes as did the first.

The wonder did not last long. In 225 BC an earthquake destroyed the town in the midst of its prosperity. Thanks to the solidarity shown by the other Greek states, Rhodes soon rose from her ruins—but not the Colossus, for the Oracle of Delphi had forbidden this. For centuries, the dislocated units of the enormous hollow carcase remained at the entrance to the port to astound travellers. They were caverns of bronze turning green, blocked by huge bricks which had formed the ballast of the statue when erect. Hellenism passed, then Byzantium and then the Arabs came. In the eighth century AD, a Jew from Emese bought the ruins. He loaded them on nine hundred camels. Nobody has ever found out what happened to the Colossus, the Jew or his caravan.

Its victory over Demetrius put the final touch to the greatness of Rhodes. It became an intellectual capital of the ancient world like Alexandria and Pergamum. It reached its peak in the Roman epoch. But no testimony to this, comparable in beauty to the monuments of the Knights, has remained in the town. The traces of the Greek walls of the temples of Dionysos and Aphrodite are archaeological small beer. On the summit of Mount St Stephen which dominates the town, surrounded by olive trees and before a vast panorama of the sea, stand the three columns of the temple of Apollo—erected with the assistance of a great deal of cement to fill in serious gaps! Near by, the steps of the stadium and its tastelessly restored pocket theatre extend below the temple in a sheltered valley where olive trees and oleanders blossom. Further on, towards the south, stretch rupestral cemeteries of the third and fourth centuries, their monumental caves hewn out of the living rock. In 1934, not far from the harbour, a statue of Venus was accidentally salvaged from the sea, whose foam once gave birth to the goddess on the shores of Cyprus. This marble phantom, white, elegant, supple, its youthful form blurred and polished by the waves, is the most graceful souvenir that pagan Rhodes has bequeathed us.

But the originality and the true charm of Rhodes are found in a labyrinth of secret streets closely girdled with formidable ramparts which form the town of the Knights. It is a complete contrast to the modern spacious, airy town stretching at ease along the straight lines of the quays and beaches, beneath trees and flowers. From a bird's-eye view, the old city forms a crescent, its horns embracing the 'closed harbour', whilst the convex part on the land side bristles with towers behind wide moats crossed by infrequent, well-guarded bridges. These enormous walls, in beautiful golden stone, constantly reinforced by the Grand Masters of the Order who marked them with their coats of arms, have lasted until the present day in an almost miraculous state of preservation—especially if one remembers that they came under Turkish artillery in three sieges and also that they were neglected for four hundred years. Inside the walls the palace of the Grand Masters, the hospital, the Lodge of St John and the Inns have suffered a great deal from dilapidation. The unfortunate results of this are only too clearly seen from sketches by travellers to the island in the eighteenth and nineteenth centuries. It is fair to say that however hateful it was for the Greek population, the Italian occupation of Rhodes had the most happy results where the monuments were concerned. With an eye to propaganda, but also with their innate good taste in restoring and giving a pleasing aspect to ruins, the Italians devoted considerable sums and a great deal of skill to preserving what could be preserved and to reconstructing as much as possible —sometimes even more. They saw to buildings undermined by vegetation, encroached on by tumbledown hovels or crumbling with old age. Underneath whitewashed roughcast they found the beautiful patina of stone taken from the quarries of Lindos. It is this activity and later the diligence of the Greek Archaeological Service—which after 1947 rapidly made good the wounds inflicted during the war—that we can thank for the opportunity of seeing the town today almost as the Knights knew it.

The Order of Knights, the Hospitallers of St John, was founded in the eleventh century by the merchants of Amalfi to shelter and protect pilgrims in the Holy Land. However, the conditions in which they had to exercise their ministry rapidly forced them to take on a military character. Alongside the purely ecclesiastical personnel, almoners and lay brothers, were also Knights recruited from almost all the countries of the West, in red habits with white crosses. When Palestine fell into the hands of the Moslems, they took refuge in Cyprus and then in Rhodes which they wrested from the declining Byzantine Empire. That was in 1309. The property of the Templars, whom the Papacy had just condemned, fell to them and these immense resources fortified their conquest. Thus the town of the Knights was born.

The Knights were divided into groups known as 'Tongues' depending on their country of origin. There were seven to begin with—the Tongues of France, of Provence, of Auvergne, of Italy, of England, of Germany and of Spain. Each Tongue was made responsible for the defence of the section of the ramparts which bore its name, and it met in a building known as an 'inn' or priory under the presidency of bailiffs or 'pillars', who together formed the chapter. At the head of the chapter stood the Grand Master of the Order, elected for life by the Knights. As the majority of the knights were French, of the eighteen Grand Masters, from Foulques de Villaret who took the town in 1309 to Villiers de l'Isle-Adam who lost it in 1522, fourteen were French, and of these the first six were from Provence. This explains why the style of the Carcassonne or Avignon buildings mixed with local elements is sometimes found in the military architecture of Rhodes.

The Knights did not shut themselves away in their beautiful ramparts. On board their galleys they swept through the pirate-infested Archipelago. They hunted the infidel in Syria, in Turkey, and even in the Peloponnese, until the capture of Constantinople in 1453, and the progress of the Turks in the Mediterranean left them isolated in the midst of the Moslem conquests. In 1480,

. *Arrivée à l'île d'Hydra.*   205. *Arrival at the island of Hydra.*   205. *Ankunft bei der Insel Hydra.*

206

206-207. Hydra. Le quai.
208. Rôtisseur de brochettes.

206-207. Hydra. The quay.
208. Spit-roasting.

206-207. Hydra. Der K
208. Hechtbraterei.

209. *Mykonos.*

210

211

212

210-211. À Mykonos. 212. Moulin de
la colline Kato Myli.

210-211. At Mykonos. 212. Mill
on the Hill of Kato Myli.

210-211. Mykonos. 212. Mü
auf dem Berge Kato Myli.

213

. *Mykonos. Eventaire de souvenirs.* 213. *Mykonos. Street stall for souvenirs.* 213. *Mykonos. Stand mit Souvenirs.*

214

215

214-215. Mykonos. Le port. En haut, la chapelle d'Hagios-Nicolaos.   214-215. Mykonos. The port. Above, the Chapel of Hagios-Nicolaos.   214-215. Mykonos. Der Ha Oben: Kapelle des Hagios Niko

6. Rue de Mykonos.   216. Street in Mykonos.   216. Straße in Mykonos.

217

217. Délos. Vue générale du site.

217. Delos. General view of the si

217. Delos. Blick über die Landschaft.

218. Délos. Maison et statue
de l'Athénienne Cléopâtre.

218. Delos. House and statue
of the Athenian Cleopatra.

218. Delos. Haus und Stati
der Athenischen Kleopa

219

9. Délos. La terrasse des
ns, œuvre des Naxiens.

219. Delos. The Terrace of Lions,
work of the Naxians.

219. Delos. Löwenterrasse,
Werk der Naxier.

220. *Délos. Torse de l'Apollon colossal des Naxiens.*

220. *Delos: body of the gigantic Apollo of the Naxians.*

220. *Delos. Torso de Kolossalstatue Apollo*

221

223

Delos. 221. Monuments votifs. 222. Temple circulaire attribué à Hermès. 223. Temple d'Isis.

Delos. 221. votive monuments. 222. The circular temple attributed to Hermes. 223. Temple of Isis.

Delos. 221. Votivmonumente. 222. Rundtempel, Hermes zugeeignet. 223. Isis-Tempel.

224

Délos.
*224. Mosaïque de
la maison de Dionysos.*

Delos.
*224. Mosaic from the
house of Dionysos.*

Delos.
*224. Mosaik des Dionyso
Hauses.*

225

*225. Mosaïque de la
maison des Dauphins.*

*225. Mosaic from the
House of the Dolphins.*

*225. Mosaik
Delphin-Hause*

226

Musée de Délos.
226. Artémis à la biche.
227. Eos enlevant Céphalos.

Museum of Delos.
226. Artemis and the doe.
227. Eos carrying off Cephalus.

Museum von Delos.
226. Artemis auf der Hirschkuh.
227. Eos, Cephalos entführend.

227

228. *Santorin.*

Crète.

229. A Héracleion.

230. Héracleion.

Fontaine de Morosini.

Crete.

229. At Heraklion.

230. Heraklion.

Fountain of Morosini.

Kreta.

229. In Heraklion.

230. Herakleion.

Morosini-Brunnen.

231

232

233

234

231-232. Héracleion. Palais de Cnossos.
Entrée nord et Propylées sud.
233. Cornes de consécration.
234. Buste de Sir Arthur Evans.

231-232. Heraklion: Palace of Knossos.
Northern entrance and southern propylaea.
233. Horns of Consecration.
234. Bust of Sir Arthur Evans.

231-232. Heraklion. Knossos-Palast.
Nordeingang und südliche Propyläen.
233. Kulthörner.
234. Büste von Sir Arthur Evans.

235. *Palais de Cnossos.*
Aire théâtrale.

235. *Palace of Knossos.*
Theatre floor.

235. *Palast von Knoss*
Theaterplatz.

36-237. Crète.

236-237. Crete.

236-237. Kreta.

Réserve de jarres.

Jars in store.

Vorrat an Krügen.

238

238. Figurine d'acrobate en ivoire. 238. Ivory figurine of an acrob.
239. Statuette en terre cuite. 239. Terra-cotta statuette.
240. Vase en forme d'oiseau 240. Bird-shaped vase from
de Kounassa. Kounassa.

238.
Akrobatische
Figur aus Elfenbein.
239.
Statuette aus
Terrakotta.
240.
Vase in Vogelform
aus Kounassa.

239   240

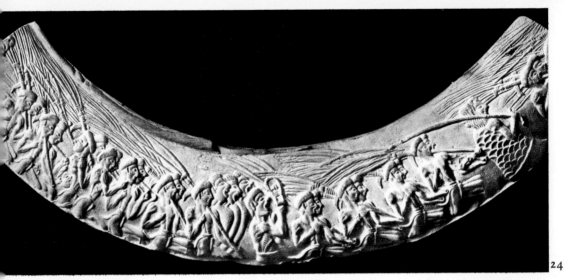

241

41. *Vase dit « des moissonneurs »*.   241. *The "harvesters" vase*.   241. *Die Schnittervase*.

42. *Figure d'argile. Adorante*   242. *Clay figure: a worshipper*   242. *Figur aus Ton*.
'*Haghia Triada*.   *from Haghia Triada*.   *Anbetende aus Hagia Triada*.

43. *Disque de Phaestos*.   243. *Disc from Phaestos*.   243. *Diskus aus Phaistos*.

242

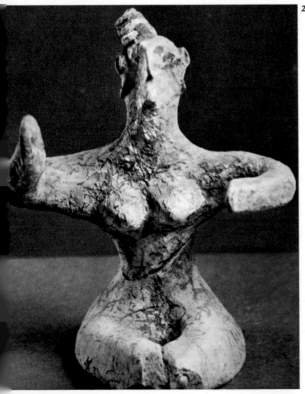

Musée d'Héracleion.

Museum of Heraklion.

Museum von Heraklion.

243

245

246

244

244. *Terra-cotta pitcher from the tombs of the Karsabas.*
245. *Jar with double axes, with stylized rosettes and leaves.*

246. *Terra-cotta vase decorat*
247. *Pitcher with stylized flower*

244. *Cruche en terre cuite provenant des tombes de Karsabas.*
245. *Jarre avec doubles haches, rosaces et feuillage stylisés.*
246. *Alabastre en terre cuite décoré d'un poulpe.*
247. *Cruche avec fleurs stylisées.*

Musée d'Héracleion.
Museum of Heraklion.
Museum von Heraklion.

an octopus. 244. *Terrakottakanne aus den Gräbern von Karsabas.* 246. *Terrakottagefäß mit Polyp.*
245. *Irdener Krug mit Äxten, Rosetten und stilisierten Blättern.* 247. *Krug mit stilisierten Blumen.*

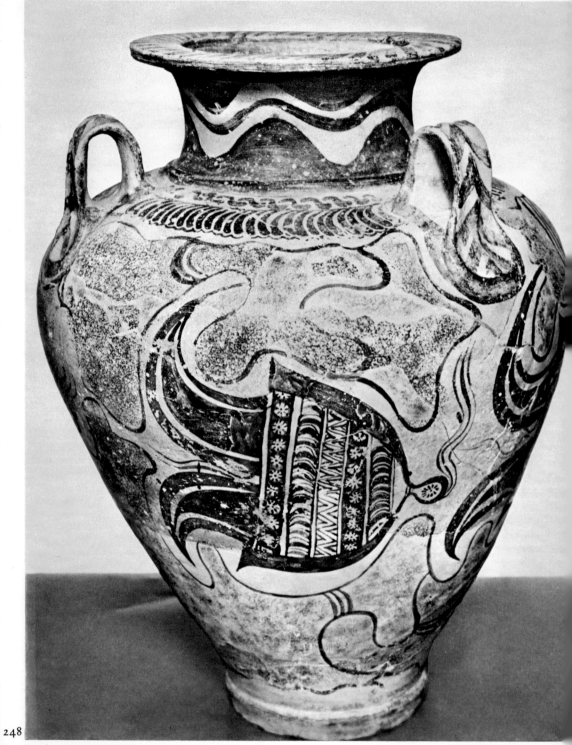

Musée d'Héracleion.

Museum of Herakli

48. Vase dit
« vase au casque ».
49. Sarcophage
d'Haghia Triada.
50. Sarcophage
e terre cuite de
alaikastro.

8. Vase known as
« the vase of the helmet ».
9. Sarcophagus from
aghia Triada.
0. Terra-cotta sarco-
agus from Palaikastro.

8. Vase, genannt
« Die Helmvase ».
9. Sarkophag aus
aghia Triada.
0. Sarkophag aus
alaikastro.

Museum von Heracleion.

251

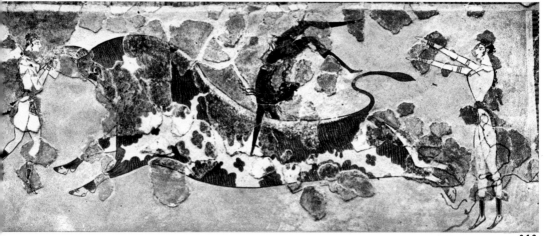

Musée d'Héracleion.

Museum of Heraklion.

Museum von Heraklion.

254   255

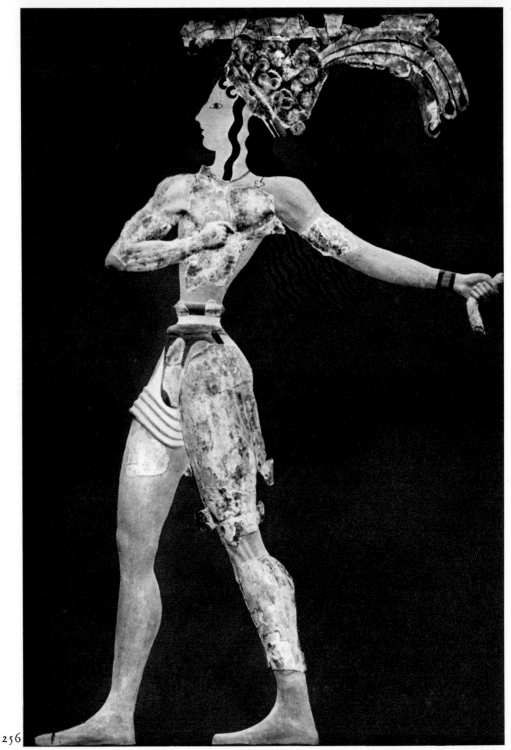

256

Musée d'Héracleion.　　　Museum of Heraklion.　　　Museum von Heraklion.

256. « Le Prince aux lys ».　256. « The prince with the lilies ».　256. « Prinz mit Lilien ».

a hundred and sixty Turkish ships appeared in front of the fortress of Rhodes. Their artillery let loose a hail of fire. The Tower of St Nicholas, struck by three hundred shells, was soon nothing but a heap of ruins. Two enormous cannon-balls penetrated the palace of the Grand Masters from the roof to the underground granaries. But the defence held out. The Turks retired.

The Knights were not content merely to repair the damage. Under the spur of three Grand Masters—Pierre d'Aubusson, Emery d'Amboise and Fabrizzio di Caretto—the fortification increased in strength and took on its present formidable appearance. The moats were widened to some hundred and twenty feet and dug to a depth of sixty feet. The thickness of the curtain walls was increased to thirty-six feet, of the parapets to twelve, whilst the firing platforms, bulwarks and false screening walls were multiplied. The gateways were given minute care. The Gate of Amboise, with its baffle plates and narrow drawbridge between two portly towers which overhang a dizzy moat, remains the most impressive success of this military art. It is grandiose and massive. Its builders have signed it with their arms in marble.

In 1522, Suleiman decided to have done with this bastion of Christianity in the heart of Islam. He organized three hundred ships and a hundred thousand men. All the previous attacks which had come to grief against the city—the siege of Poliorcetes, the great siege of 1480—were nothing in comparison with this final battle when both attackers and defenders gave proof of equal desperation. A thousand cannons bombarded the town without respite, spreading terror everywhere. They struck the ramparts, already sapped and mined, which were rebuilt amidst ruined houses as quickly as they were destroyed, whilst the attackers sacrificed entire units in places in filling the ditches with earth. Four successive assaults were broken. Suleiman, discouraged, only gained his victory through the treachery of one of the Knights who, piqued at not having been elected Grand Master, came to revive his hopes. On December 22, 1522, a final assault took the town by sheer weight of numbers. The Knights were granted a respite of twelve days to quit the island. Escorted by four thousand inhabitants who preferred exile to the Ottoman yoke, they left Rhodes on January 1, 1523, for the island of Malta where they afterwards remained.

Under Turkish domination, Rhodes slowly fell into slumber, although the natural advantages of its position and the resources of its soil maintained a certain prosperity. The old emblazoned cannons rusted uselessly on the ramparts, while several charming mosques, their stumpy domes flanked by the slender shanks of the minarets, were built in the city. Outside the ramparts great Moslem cemeteries stood peacefully in the shade, their disordered white stones pointing in all directions. Fearing the impatience of their subjects, the Turkish officials obliged them to retire each evening outside the walls when the shooting of a cannon proclaimed the closing of the gates. Only the Jews were authorized to remain in the ghetto. These precautions prevented the inhabitants of Rhodes from participating in the liberating revolution of 1821. As in neighbouring Crete, they remained under the Ottoman yoke until Italian troops landed on the island at the time of the Italo-Turkish conflict. Rhodes then thought herself on the verge of liberty, but she had only changed her master. The Treaty of Lausanne which ended the Italo-Turkish war in 1912 stipulated that Turkey could recover the island after the evacuation of Libya and Tripolitania. The war of 1914 postponed the application of the treaty and the Italians remained on the island, for good or ill, until 1947. Rhodes then returned to the Greek community, from which it had been officially separated since 1309.

At Rhodes, more than anywhere else in Greece, each phase of history is alive in the monuments that it has bequeathed. The often strange *rapprochement* of different styles gives the city an original and attractive appearance. The Inns of France, of Auvergne and of Provence, the coats of arms with their fleurs-de-lys, the names of the Grand Masters—all evoke at the other end of the Mediterranean old memories of some corner of old France. And that is true despite the palm trees and the banana trees, sleepy mosques beside singing fountains underneath some vast plane tree, amidst all the poetry of the Orient. The historic monuments, restored, dusted, surrounded by disciplined flowers, manifestly cry out for admiration from the tourist and bear witness to the fact that the Italians have passed that way. They have left a strong imprint on the new city. The official buildings built in stone from Lindos in mediaeval style are somewhat ostentatious, but they mingle happily with their surroundings. The palaces by the side of the sea, the villas with Venetian shutters surrounded by exuberant gardens, the tarred roads edged with flowery pavements, are far more reminiscent of the Riviera or some corner of the Côte d'Azur than of the usual Greek province. And yet the rhythm of life, a certain gaiety, and the transparency of the atmosphere which brings all these disparate factors into a luminous unity is proof that Greece is here in this island where history has left such a rich heritage.

Inside the old city a climbing road joins the hospital of the Knights to the palace of the Grand Masters. The hospital is a magnificent monument and contains the collections of the Museum of Rhodes. An ogival portico surrounds the central sun-drenched courtyard with its shady arcades, whence a wide open staircase, compact in its geometrical bareness, leads up to the first storey. The long hall with two arches, refectory or covered walk, preserves a freshness beneath its elegant ribs that is welcome to the tourist, overcome by heat.

In a silence only broken by the re-echo of its paving-stones, the Street of the Knights leads from the hospital to the palace of the Grand Masters. It passes in turn in front of the Inn of Italy and the Inn of the Tongue of France, near a small church with an ogival portico, followed by the residence of the chaplain of the Tongue of France. Then comes the Inn of the Tongue of Spain, the gallery of which crosses the road like a bridge, and the Inn of the Tongue of Provence. The terraced roofs are edged with merlons, the façades flat, the stone a beautiful yellow on which the marble of the coats of arms stands out; there is a mysterious darkness in the interior courtyards. The eye is charmed, while in the atmosphere of calm, history seems to be contemplating itself. Narrow streets, where houses stand shoulder to shoulder linked by buttresses, converge on the Citadel Square. It is tempting to let oneself be absorbed in their mystery. The palace of the Grand Masters, dominating the square with its enormous square silhouette, like the hospital of the Knights welcomes the visitor to a vast courtyard, which is bordered by a gallery, reached by a monumental staircase. A fortress inside a fortress, this superb building dominates the modern city of which one can see the market place or *mandraki* amidst thick vegetation. Its whiteness is dazzling. The vast quay where rises the campanile of the church of the Evanghelismos built to the plan of St John of the Knights, looking so new though in ancient style, is also visible.

The tour of the ramparts is undoubtedly the most beautiful promenade in Rhodes, as much because of the ramparts themselves, for their mass and size can be better understood this way, as for the spectacle they provide. Outside the moats, patches of green and gardens shade the avenues on the site of the Turkish cemeteries. The flat-roofed houses of the old city stretch out at the foot of the palace of the Grand Masters, with narrow streets winding between them. The minarets of the mosques, the sails of the windmills and the green gardens add charm to the stern rectangular aspect of the ensemble. Towards the sea, one overlooks the calm waters of the 'closed port', 'the most beautiful and the largest along all the road to Jerusalem'. Here one also sees the long jetty which is terminated by the fort of St Nicholas, bordered by painted caiques; and the bustle of the modern town which does not shake the torpor of the city of the Knights.

An excellent network of roads makes it possible to visit the remainder of the island in comfort and also the sites of the Dorian cities with sonorous names such as Ialysos, Camiros and Lindos. Ialysos is quite near. The road runs along the western side across the plain which surrounds the agricultural hamlet of Trianda. It is a pleasant plain like all fertile Greek plains. The houses scattered amidst the abundance of orchards recall, in contrast to the western style of Rhodes, the familiar appearance of the Greek houses, painted white and blue. The white sails of hundreds of windmills turn in the sky, unceasingly pumping water to maintain this prosperity.

Soon, the road winds along the sides of Mount Filerimo on whose summit the acropolis of Ialysos once stood. The slopes sheltered by pine trees and cedars rise suddenly above the plain. You seem to be standing at a dizzy height above it when you have barely climbed some eight or nine hundred feet above sea level. Hardly anything remains of the temple of Athena Ialysia other than its foundations and occasional bits of a Doric frieze stretched out on the soil in front of the church of the Knights, which is embellished with a large Maltese cross. The castle itself has been restored on such a scale that it seems to be new. Around a large well in the central courtyard, stone galleries unfold with their beautiful yellow stone-colouring, brightened by the brilliance of bougainvillaeas. All this forms a somewhat artificial framework—it might even be called false— but it is exquisite. A splendid panorama is visible from the upper gallery with its flattened arches—the plain of Trianda and its Orchard of Eden, dominated to the north by the city of Rhodes, powdered by a faint haze, a spot of light against the intense blue of the sea.

On the southern slope of the mountain, a rough path overgrown with wild grass and thistles leads in a few minutes to the pretty Doric Fountain of Ialysos, backing on to the rock from which it drew its water in days of yore. It is one of the most complete remaining to us from Greek antiquity. Its elegant pilasters speckled with sunshine through the wavy foliage even today seem to exude freshness, although it has long since ceased to flow.

The originality of Camiros is that for once the architecture of the Knights is missing. The purely classical ruins of the city stand in the hollow of a picturesque valley not far from the sea. The uninitiated have difficulty in finding their way in the meanderings of the ruins. One is more clearly able to follow their arrangement by viewing them from the top of the acropolis. This is planted with pine trees; their twisted trunks contrasting with the slender columns of a Doric portico are the delight of photographers in search of a foreground.

Whatever their charm, neither Ialysos nor Camiros can compare in beauty with the luminous city of Lindos. After Rhodes, it is the city that makes the strongest impression on the visitor. It took pride in being the home of Chares the sculptor, whose fame lasted longer than the bronze of his famous Colossus. Its strategic value as an observation post on the eastern coast and the excellence of its harbour did not escape the attention of the Knights. They erected a powerful castle on the ancient acropolis, defended by a Greek garrison under the orders of twelve of the Knights. The Greek population never experienced the same feelings of resentment or hatred towards the Knights that it nourished elsewhere against foreign occupiers, the Crusaders, Venetians, or Genoese, to whom it even preferred the Turks. The activity of their order was altruistic, devoted to the defence of a common faith and not to trade, the profits of which went to Genoa or Venice, with the burden falling on the Greeks. Mutual confidence linked the Knights and the people of Rhodes. After the fall of the island, many of the latter preferred to go into exile with the vanquished rather than remain in their country under the yoke of new masters.

The landscape of Lindos, burning with life beneath an African sky, strikes the visitor by the sheer mass of its crenellated acropolis. A flat rock surface crowned with ramparts from which a temple emerges, when seen from the west it evokes the outline of the acropolis of Athens. A prow sculptured in the rock at the foot of the ascent recalls the glories of the sailors of Rhodes whose vessels carried, with the amphorae of wine with their stamped handles, oil, cypress wood and those beautiful silver coins marked with the arms of the island—the rose on the obverse and on the reverse the head of the sun surrounded by rays—along all the periphery of the Mediterranean. A narrow staircase clinging first to the side of the rock and then to the mediaeval rampart leads to the fortified gateway of the acropolis. The visitor crosses the shade of the arcade and then stops—bewildered, blinded—on the edge of the sundrenched esplanade. The eye first distinguishes the outline of the small church of St John; then a confusion of ruined walls, the palace of the Commandant; then finally, the Hellenistic portico, its wings framing a monumental staircase, silhouetting against the sky the austerity of its geometric outlines, as precise as a design on a drawing-board. Each stair is underlined with a ray of sun and the spectator first imagines that it leads to nowhere but the blue sky above. But as he climbs further he sees the entablature and then the columns of the temple of Athena Lindia, the communal sanctuary of all the people of Rhodes. He approaches the parapet which edges the temple. Cut as if by a gigantic sabre, the red rock falls vertically into unmoving, crystal waves at the base of a three hundred and fifty foot precipice. From the northern extremity of the acropolis he has a bird's-eye view of the white town crossed by dark streets and transmuted by the play of light so as to follow the rules of a delicate cubism. The harbour looks like a round blue basin. Brightly coloured caiques sleep along the quays. Others are drawn up on the sand of the beach, in front of the cafés frequented by customers whose presence one can only guess at in the shade of the reed screens.

It is banal but almost compulsory to praise the luminosity of the Greek sky. On this acropolis exposed to all the torches of the solstice, in the great blaze of sunshine, lighting and consuming a thousand flashing lights on the peaceful roof of the sea, in the silence of the necropolis bathing the antique monuments, a gentle torpor invades the mind.

Descending into the town we are lost in the network of narrow streets. We go into one of the houses. The interior, let us be honest, has been dressed up for our benefit. What does it matter? The courtyard paved with pebbles, the flowers, the well and the beautiful stone façade whose ogive preserves the tradition of the architecture of the Knights long after their departure, all this has an authentic charm—as well as the *glyko* and the glass of water misted with fresh condensation that the visitor is always offered. On the wall, faience of Lindos colours the half-light with its blues, greens and beautiful ripe-tomato reds. On the ancient bed, we see the fine curtains embroidered with red and green, the *sperveria*, conveying all the pride of a trousseau handed down from generation to generation.

The boat leaves Rhodes behind. We throw a last glance at the withdrawn city of the Knights and the modern city with its welcoming avenues. We try to analyse the mixed but vivid impressions we take away. It was part of the destiny of this Dorian island to find renown in the military and in the colossal. Sculptors erecting bronze colossi in the port, in public places and in temple courtyards (Pliny could still see hundreds of them), ramparts to match epic sieges—both history itself and the monuments prevent one forgetting this aspect of the genius of Rhodes. And yet, it is in thinking of the abundance of flowers, the beautiful patina of the stones lit by the purple of the bougainvillaeas, the sails of a windmill found unexpectedly at the turn of a street, of the sky over Lindos, that the visitor recalls the two words of Horace, mistranslating the adjective without a twinge of remorse, *Clara Rhodos*.

*
* *

To leave Greece is to take away with one as many regrets as enchanting memories. What one has seen makes one want to see even more and never makes up for the sacrifices one had to consent to. Many famous names have not been mentioned in this book. We have neglected Corfu and its Italianate beauty, Mytilene and Chios, Patmos with its square houses dominated by the red mass of its fortified monastery, Cos and Carpathos whose picturesque landscape perhaps surpasses even that of the Cyclades, and Skyros with its peasant dwellings carved in wood. One would have to sail for ten years like Ulysses in this endless archipelago. In Greece itself, we have passed by many places. Mount Taygetus and Messenia, the Palace of Nestor overlooking the vineyards and Navarino Bay, and the towns of the north on the shores of their lakes—all these places deserved longer visits. But Greece the country in the world which is least suited to the hasty tourist. In order to be understood, its landscape demands a certain familiarity, a certain idleness, a certain unhurriedness. Only then will it reveal all its charms. To a hurried visitor, Epidaurus will never be anything but a field of ruins beneath its thistles. Only those who know how to 'pass by', as they say in Greece, can understand the harmony and see the bees beneath its pines.

The charm of Greece is made up of its light, of its contrasting scenery, of the memories of a past which constantly enrich the spectacle of the present. There is also a certain atmosphere of liberty and of congeniality which gives the journey an unusual enjoyment. The triumph of Greek hospitality is that when in Greece one feels at home. The Greeks say 'Europe' when they talk of the countries of the West, as if they themselves were not part of it. None the less, when the traveller lands in Piraeus or on the aerodrome at Athens when returning from the Middle East, he definitely feels he is entering a familiar world. The community of civilization is not an empty word. The long humanistic tradition on which we draw, through study, gives every man here, even if illiterate, the desire to know other men and to welcome them fittingly. The Greeks are part of our family. We can go to them as to our cousins in the south. In their language they have a word that is difficult to translate, a word that expresses their courtesy, a word that is on the lips of the shoe-shine boys, of the merchant, of the taxi-driver, of the monk who offers you a *glyko* at the entrance to his monastery, of the Athenian bourgeois and of the minister. This word is *oriste*, i.e., 'make yourself at home here, come in and sit down, what can we do for you?' This is the word one hears most frequently on one's journey. The word that remains with the traveller on his voyage home, an invitation to return . . . .

257

57. *Rhodes.*
cropropole de Lindos.

257. *Rhodes.*
The Acropolis of Lindos.

257. *Rhodos.*
Akropolis von Lindos.

258

258. *Acropole de Lindos. Grand Portique.*

258. *Acropolis of Lindos: great portic*

258. Große Säulenhalle der Akropolis von Lindos.

259

259. *Ialysos. Eglise des Chevaliers et vestiges du temple antique.*   259. *Ialysos. Church of the Knigh*

260. *Cloître de l'Hôpital des Chevaliers. Musée actuel.*   260. *Cloister of the Hospital of th*

261

and remains of the ancient temple.   *259. Ialysos. Kirche der Ritter und Spuren des antiken Tempels.*

Knights, now a museum.   *260. Kreuzgang des Ordenshospitals, jetzt Museum.*

261. *Rue des Chevaliers:*
auberge de Provence.
262. *Auberge de France.*
263. *Pavage byzantin.*

261. *Street of the Knights:*
Inn of Provence.
262. *Inn of France.*
263. *Byzantine paving.*

261. *Straße der Ritter,*
Provençalische Herberge.
262. *Französische Herberge.*
263. *Byzantinisches Pflastersteinmosaik.*

262

263

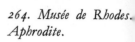

264. Musée de Rhodes.
Aphrodite.

264. Museum of Rhodes
Aphrodite.

264. Museum von Rhodos.
Aphrodite.

264

INDEX

Names of persons, or characters from Greek theogony, are in italics, unless they refer to a work of art. Numerals in bold type refer to plate numbers of illustrations

297

Index